HOW SCHOOLS REALLY MATTER

HOW
SCHOOLS
REALLY
MATTER

WHY OUR ASSUMPTION
ABOUT SCHOOLS AND
INEQUALITY IS
MOSTLY WRONG

Douglas B. Downey

THE UNIVERSITY OF CHICAGO PRESS
Chicago and London

The University of Chicago Press, Chicago 60637
The University of Chicago Press, Ltd., London
© 2020 by The University of Chicago
Published 2020
Printed in the United States of America

29 28 27 26 25 24 23 22 21 20   1 2 3 4 5

ISBN-13: 978-0-226-73319-7 (cloth)
ISBN-13: 978-0-226-73322-7 (paper)
ISBN-13: 978-0-226-73336-4 (e-book)
DOI: https://doi.org/10.7208/chicago/9780226733364.001.0001

Library of Congress Cataloging-in-Publication Data

Names: Downey, Douglas B., author.
Title: How schools really matter : why our assumption about
schools and inequality is mostly wrong / Douglas B. Downey.
Description: Chicago : University of Chicago Press, 2020.
| Includes bibliographical references and index.
Identifiers: LCCN 2020007858 | ISBN 9780226733197 (cloth) |
ISBN 9780226733227 (paperback) | ISBN 9780226733364 (ebook)
Subjects: LCSH: Educational equalization—United
States. | Public schools—United States.
Classification: LCC LC213.2 .D69 2020 | DDC 379.2/6—dc23
LC record available at https://lccn.loc.gov/2020007858
♾ This paper meets the requirements of
ANSI/NISO Z39.48-1992 (Permanence of Paper).

*For Eddie and Wanda Downey, who gave
me a wonderful early childhood*

CONTENTS

INTRODUCTION

The prevailing view about schools and inequality in America goes like this—*children learn more in schools serving high-income and white children than in schools serving low-income and minority children.* (Throughout the book I will refer to "inequality" in schools and outside of schools.) Rich parents believe it's true—it's part of why they pay for their children to attend private schools or buy homes in wealthy neighborhoods with "good" public schools. Poor parents believe it's true too—it's why they support school reform and sometimes enroll their children in charter schools. The story is so widely accepted that it has become a cultural assumption and can now be asserted without evidence.

But what if this assumption is wrong and children attending schools serving advantaged and disadvantaged children learn about the same amount? Part of why we feel so confident about the traditional story is because we can see with our own eyes how some schools have more resources than others. We see white kids going to the new school with the computer lab and black kids going to the aging school without one. Or the local newspaper reports that the reading and math test scores at the rich kids' school are much higher than the scores at the poor kids' school. Could all of this evidence really be wrong? And could the parents who spend so much time and energy making sure their children get into the "good" schools really be wasting their time?

This book is about evaluating the old evidence, considering

new evidence, and developing a more accurate understanding of schools and inequality. The traditional story isn't completely wrong. There are significant disparities in resources between the schools advantaged and disadvantaged children attend, a problem that requires attention. But there is good reason to believe that the traditional story is not quite right because several important patterns don't fit. If schools serving advantaged children are substantially better than the ones serving disadvantaged children, we should observe that achievement gaps between high- and low-income children grow when school is in session, yet they do not. This contrary pattern needs to receive more attention and the traditional story needs to be reevaluated. We should do this not as a way to let schools off the hook but rather to identify accurately when and why achievement gaps emerge. That's the best way to reduce them.

I started doubting The Assumption one spring afternoon in 1992. That day I was minding my own business, working on my dissertation at Indiana University, when my adviser, Brian Powell, recommended that I read the article "Summer Setback" written by Doris Entwisle and Karl Alexander, two Johns Hopkins researchers.[1] How often do you read something and then end up changing your mind about how the world works? What I read in that article shaped my intellectual journey during the next quarter century. The authors made the provocative claim that schools are compensatory—helping the disadvantaged *more* than the advantaged.

What they showed was simple—gaps in math skills between children from high- and low-income families in Baltimore grew during the summers, when school was out, but not during the school years. The summer patterns were no surprise. Of course, children from advantaged families learn more because they enjoy more stable home environments with educated parents, health care, good nutrition, and trips to the library. The shocker was the school-year results. Children from high- and low-income families learned at the same rate when school was in session! How could that happen if the disadvantaged kids were experiencing both poorer family environments and poorer schools? After finishing their article I'll admit that I didn't immediately change my perspective—I still viewed schools as playing a significant role exacerbating inequality. I figured there had to be something wrong with the Baltimore study. My conversion toward Entwisle and Alexander's thinking about schools was not an epiphany but more of a process, like Elisabeth Kübler-Ross's stages of grieving (denial, anger, bargaining, depression, acceptance). I'm sure there was denial and anger in there, maybe some bargaining. This book is about how I eventually got to the acceptance stage, believing that our ideas about schools and inequality need to be rethought.

Part of why it took a long time to shift my position is that the traditional view, that schools are an engine of inequality, seems to be supported by most research. In graduate school studying sociology, I was exposed to a wide range of studies demonstrating how kids from wealthy families enjoy much better schools than those from poor families. For example, in Jonathan Kozol's *Savage Inequalities*, he colorfully describes the unequal resources across schools serving advantaged and disadvantaged children.[2] Advantaged children were taught by better teachers and enjoyed newer curriculums, more abundant extracurriculars, and safer school environments. Kozol described the overcrowding in schools serving poor black children, the racial segregation of the schools, and the deteriorating physical condition of the buildings. If reading about it doesn't persuade, one can see the large differences in a film I show my undergraduate students, *Children in America's Schools*, which contrasts the new and high-tech facilities for the children in wealthy Dublin, Ohio, versus the schools lacking art, physical education, and even computers in the southeastern Appalachian section of the state.[3]

In addition, several scholars argued that, even when attending the same schools, advantaged children had it better. For example, they pointed to evidence that children from wealthy families are more frequently placed in high-ability reading groups or the college track classes, even when their skills didn't merit the placement, and teachers have higher expectations for children from advantaged versus disadvantaged backgrounds. This literature and my gut both told me that school quality matters a great deal, that advantaged children enjoy much better schools than disadvantaged children, and that all of this explained an important part of inequality. The Baltimore study was probably just odd.

Then, in the early 2000s, the Department of Education released the *Early Childhood Longitudinal Study* (ECLS-K:1998), new data that would allow a substantially better examination of the Baltimore patterns. There were lots of nationally representative datasets of American students already available but this one had a unique feature—rather than simply observe children once every year or two like most studies, children were observed at the beginnings and ends of consecutive school years. This data collection schedule turns out to be like gold for researchers interested in understanding how schools matter, because it allows them to link children's scores at the end of one year to the beginning of another and estimate how much they learned during a summer. For the first time we would have nationally representative data of American children that would allow us to observe how inequality *changed* when school was in versus out. Now we could test whether the Baltimore patterns would repeat in national data (see appendix A for a more thorough description of the ECLS-K data).

Our research team at Ohio State turned its attention to the big question—does inequality grow faster when school is in or out—and we expected to show how schools make inequality worse. But a funny thing happened on the way to refuting the Baltimore sociologists. It turned out that the patterns from the nationally representative ECLS-K dataset were largely similar to those in Baltimore: gaps in skills between high- and low-income children grew faster when school was out versus in. Rather than refuting the provocative Baltimore patterns, the national data replicated them.

We published those results in a 2004 article entitled "Are Schools the 'Great Equalizer'?,"[4] but that study left us with a puzzle. If gaps in reading and math skills didn't increase much when school was in session, were the schools serving advantaged children really any better than the schools serving disadvantaged children? It sure seems like they are but the seasonal patterns challenged that idea, at least with respect to how much children learn reading and math in schools. To really know, though, we would need to carefully isolate school effects on children's learning from the pervasive influence of families and neighborhoods.

In another study published in 2008 ("Are 'Failing' Schools Really Failing?"), we considered how evaluations of schools change as we use techniques that better isolate how schools matter. We introduced a new way of approaching this issue—the difference between summer learning and school-year learning—to identify schools' impact on children's learning independent of their nonschool environments. We showed how, when schools are evaluated this way, our notions of which ones are "failing" change in important ways. The provocative conclusion from that paper was that advantaged children were not enjoying any more school-based learning than disadvantaged children.[5]

We thought we had just transformed the world by showing that schools do more to reduce than increase inequality and that there is virtually no difference in the amount of school-based learning occurring in schools serving advantaged versus disadvantaged children. Both papers were published in prestigious journals, garnered national awards, and have been well-cited.

But the world didn't change much. Education research largely continued as it had. For example, the opening paragraph of the latest *Handbook of the Sociology of Education for the 21st Century* states: "We need to understand why the educational needs of those with limited economic and social resources remain unheeded while the institutions that serve them remain woefully inadequate."[6] Similarly, in the 2017 edition of the leading sociology of education textbook for college students (*Schools and Society: A Sociological Approach to Education*), the six readings in the "Who Gets Ahead? Race, Class, and Gender in Education" section all emphasized ways in which schools reproduce or exacerbate inequality.[7] And nearly all of the graduate students who came to study education issues with me at Ohio State continued to want to understand schools' pernicious effects. Our publications had undermined one of sociology of education's main questions—How do schools make inequality worse?— and yet the band played on. The view that schools generate inequality continued to dominate the way scholars thought, and our work had little influence on this narrative.

Of course, the evidence that schools are compensatory was not (and is not) indisputable, part of why there should be debate. It is stronger in some studies than others, better documented in the early grades than later ones, demonstrated most clearly among cognitive skills and less so among other outcomes, stronger for income-based achievement gaps than race-based ones, and reliant on assumptions. But all evidence has limitations and it turns out that the limitations from seasonal comparison studies are considerably more modest than the limitations supporting the view that children learn more in schools serving advantaged children. A thoughtful approach weighs the merits of evidence on both sides. Admittedly, the seasonal evidence was too new and modest to completely overturn the dominant view about schools and inequality, but it seemed like it was not influencing scholars much at all.

I worried that The Assumption might be wrong and that our field was providing poor advice to policymakers. We were spending considerable energy trying to figure out how to improve the schools serving disadvantaged students. It's not that this was a bad thing to do, it's just that it was unlikely to be the optimal way forward to reducing achievement gaps and, ultimately, reducing inequality in broader society. In addition, a distorted understanding of what generates and maintains achievement gaps could undermine efforts to reduce inequality in society at large. Education scholars could and should study processes within schools that make inequality worse, but I thought that they should acknowledge the evidence showing that schools' *overall* effect on cognitive skills was neutral or even compensatory and engage it in debate. They weren't doing that.

When it comes to understanding schools and inequality, the dominant narrative about how the world works (schools increase inequality) may be one of those strongly held beliefs that is not easily modified. It's so widely endorsed that it has become a cultural assumption. This may be in part because of the Hollywood narrative about schools portrayed in films like *Stand and Deliver* and *Waiting for Superman*—disadvantaged children typically enduring poor teachers—but it's also due to the mountain of research evidence that seems to support the dominant narrative about schools. I'll show in part I of this book, however, that the mountain is merely correlational. As soon as we ask for causal evidence, the mountain collapses. While we observe large differences in the math and reading skills between advantaged and disadvantaged children, the best evidence indicates that these gaps have little to do with schools.

This book is not the first to challenge the dominant narrative about schools. In 1966, most people thought that schools made inequality worse because of the unequal distribution of resources, part of the reason the Department of Education commissioned James Coleman, a highly respected sociologist, to study this issue. But the massive *Equality of Opportunity*, better known as the Coleman Report, famously concluded that inequality in math and reading skills comes primarily from families and that schools play only a small role, a pattern Jencks and colleagues replicated.[8] Social scientists have been arguing about the Coleman Report for the last half century. Critics of Coleman point out, correctly, that his report had a weak claim to causality because it only observed children at one point in time.[9]

Inspired by Coleman's and Jencks's work, this book extends the discussion about schools and inequality in two ways. First, rather than continue the debate about whether schools play a large or small role in increasing inequality, this book expands the discussion considerably by presenting a challenging new possibility—that schools reduce some dimensions of inequality. To date, academics have not given the possibility that schools are compensatory serious theoretical consideration. Indeed, when I discuss schools' potential compensatory mechanisms in chapter 4, I will have little help from previous scholars. They just haven't thought much about this.

Second, this book relies on unique evidence that more powerfully demonstrates schools' role than the evidence available to Coleman and Jencks. Correlation does not necessarily mean causation, but it turns out that while this was a weakness of both Coleman's and Jencks's work, the way it distorted their conclusions was much different than how most detractors thought. Critics thought that better research designs would show that schools increase inequality. Instead, better research designs reveal that not only do schools play little role increasing inequality, they may reduce it in some ways. The better research designs I'm talking about are the seasonal comparison studies I described above, where we see how inequality grows faster when school is out versus in.

The seasonal research is also complemented by another pattern that is growing in consensus. It turns out that gaps in skills between advantaged and disadvantaged children are largely formed prior to kindergarten entry and then do not grow appreciably when children are in school. Indeed, a large proportion of achievement gaps are in place by kindergarten entry.[10] Much of the "action" of inequality therefore occurs very early in life. Combine this pattern with the seasonal results and it's clear that the engine behind inequality lies outside of schools.

So those are the empirical patterns that prompted me to revise my thinking about schools. I now agree with Karl Alexander that when it comes to inequality, schools are "more 'part of the solution' than 'part of the problem.'"[11] This shift in thinking has resulted in a corresponding decline in my enthusiasm for school-based reforms as a way of combatting achievement gaps. That is not to say that school reform has no role. Schools currently play a meaningful role reducing inequality in some outcomes and some school reforms might reduce inequality further. Like many others, I view it as unconscionable that some schools are filled with iPads while others lack basic resources because it violates the American value that everyone has a chance if they try hard. Your chances are diminished if your school's resources are way below those of others.[12]

But a clear-eyed understanding of how schools currently matter reveals the limitations of their role. At its worst, school reform is a distraction from the more fundamental changes we need to reduce inequality—a sandbox to play in while the serious battles are fought elsewhere. School reform efforts might even make the problem worse because they can end up bolstering The Assumption, prompting high-resource parents to concentrate in high-status neighborhoods in hopes of providing their children with the best schools. These moves probably do much less to advantage their children in terms of learning than the parents think, but they do lead to greater residential segregation by income and race and greater polarization regarding our shared values.

If we are serious about reducing achievement gaps, we will need to reduce the inequality we have allowed to develop *outside* of schools—the income inequality that has been increasing over the last few decades. Some might argue that we can't control that—it's a product of markets, globalization, and technological growth. I agree that it is affected by those forces, but it is not determined by them. As a group of University of California–Berkeley sociologists put it, the level of inequality we have in society is partly "by design"—it is a result of the policy choices we make.[13] We could make those decisions differently. Other countries have made different decisions, and they have less economic stratification and more highly skilled students on average.[14]

We need meaningful reform of the distribution of rewards in broader society, which will require fundamental policy change. Of course, that's a substantially more difficult problem than reforming schools. Many academics I talk to argue that we can't do anything about inequality in broader society and so we should just focus on schools. I wrote this book because I disagree with that position. I believe that by developing an accurate understanding of schools' role in society, we will be better positioned to garner the public enthusiasm needed for addressing the root sources of inequality outside of schools.

Part I

WHY WE SHOULDN'T BE BLAMING SCHOOLS SO MUCH

CHAPTER 1

The Forgotten 87 Percent

HERBERT WALBERG'S OUTRAGEOUS CLAIM

I'm in my office reading a 1984 article by Herbert Walberg published in *Phi Delta Kappan* and I've just come across a sentence I know is wrong. "No way is that true!," I say out loud. The offending sentence reads: "The 12 years of school, each year made up of 180 six-hour days, add up to 12,960 hours, or about 13% of the waking life of a youngster's first 18 years."[1]

I'm sure that this shockingly low number is wrong. I'd bet my house on it. I drive my two kids to and from school all the time. There's just no way that at age 18 they will have spent only 13 percent of their waking hours in school. I get out a calculator to prove Walberg wrong. I immediately note that my kids went to kindergarten, so they will attend 13 years of school, not 12 like Walberg's estimate. And my kids are in school for 6.5 hours a day, not just 6, so there. This Walberg guy is so wrong I'm thinking as I start cranking out the math.

But then I get my final number for my son Nicholas. Hmmmm. My estimate is that Nicholas will have spent 15.9 percent of his waking hours in school by the time he's 18.[2] My percentage is a little higher than Walberg's because of the additional schooling (kindergarten) and a slightly longer school day, but the conclusion is the same—kids are in school WAY less than most of us think.

TRYING TO UNDERSTAND HOW SCHOOLS MATTER WHEN YOU HAVE AN EIGHT-HUNDRED-POUND GORILLA PROBLEM

When I present the fact that children are in school such a limited percentage of their life, most people are surprised. But for anyone interested in understanding how schools matter, they should keep Walberg's 87 percent (the percentage of waking hours *not* spent in school) in mind. It reminds us that when we're trying to understand how some aspect of children's development is influenced by schools, we can't forget that children mostly aren't there—they're at home and in their neighborhoods. Even if some children go to school a little more than Walberg's estimate (mine do), it's not by much. Unless the kid is at a boarding school, the vast majority of their waking hours are spent outside of school.

That means that there is an eight-hundred-pound gorilla in the mix, the home and neighborhood, making it difficult to understand schools' role. The high reading test scores at East Elementary may be because of the great teachers, or they may be because of what children experience during the 87 percent of time they aren't there. And maybe the low reading test scores at Pleasant Street Elementary are due to lousy teachers at the school, but they also could be low in spite of the school. It's hard to know.

Most people have a general sense that schools aren't completely responsible for their students' outcomes. We know that some schools face tougher challenges than others, serving children who come in with poorer skills and home environments that are less conducive to supporting learning. But we don't really understand how big a deal this is because we make two errors. First, we underestimate how much early childhood shapes children's skills and learning trajectories. This is surprising because it seems like there is constant news about the importance of the first three years of life. Nevertheless, most people don't realize that achievement gaps between advantaged and disadvantaged children are mostly formed prior to kindergarten. Second, most people overestimate how much schools matter. I don't mean that they overestimate how much schools influence learning—children really do learn much faster in school versus out—but that they overestimate how much schools influence *inequality* in skills. It turns out that when we study achievement gaps carefully, and by carefully I mean taking seriously the eight-hundred-pound gorilla problem, our ideas about how much schools contribute to inequality change in important ways. It becomes clear that schools play a much more limited role than we thought. Indeed, in some ways they even rub the rough edges off inequality.

But we don't develop a clear understanding of how schools matter unless we keep Walberg in mind, acknowledging the 87 percent of waking time when children are not in school. This huge confound can really distort our understanding. This point is critical because it influences the kind of research best equipped for addressing the problem. When there are such huge differences in the kinds of students one school serves versus another, it is very difficult to understand how the schools matter by simply trying to "statistically control" for differences between the students. Not only do eight-hundred-pound gorillas get to sleep wherever they want, they are too big to statistically control.

CHAPTER 2
Chickens, Eggs, and Achievement Gaps

WHEN DO ACHIEVEMENT GAPS EMERGE?

In the spring of 2010, I realized I had a problem. I had just come across a graph produced by James Heckman, the Nobel Prize–winning economist from the University of Chicago, showing how gaps in reading and math skills (between children with college-educated mothers versus mothers who were high-school dropouts) were large at age three and only increased a bit (about ten percent) by age eighteen. Surprisingly, nearly the entire achievement gap was in place before schools had a chance to matter. This was a problem because a large part of my academic field (sociology of education) is built around understanding how schools reproduce or exacerbate inequality. If achievement gaps are nearly entirely formed during early childhood and then hardly grow once school starts, it's hard to see how schools could be the culprits we thought they were.

Of course, just seeing one graph in someone's article, even if that someone is a Nobel Prize winner, doesn't mean it's true. When I come across patterns with such major consequences I want to make sure I can believe them. I spent the next few days exploring whether Heckman's graph would replicate in one of the highest quality nationally representative datasets available:

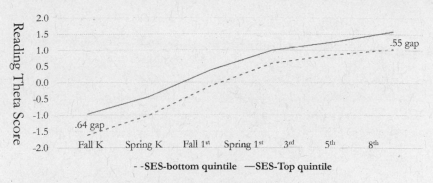

FIGURE 2.1. Socioeconomic gaps in reading skills narrow between kindergarten and eighth grade. ECLS-K:1998.

The Early Childhood Longitudinal Study—Kindergarten Cohort of 1998 (ECLS-K:98).

Figure 2.1 plots the gap in reading skills between children from the top fifth in socioeconomic status or SES (a composite of household income, parents' education, and occupational prestige) versus those from the bottom fifth. The first thing to note is that children from high-SES families consistently outperform those from low-SES families at every grade level (no surprise). You can see that by eighth grade, high-SES children are 0.55 reading scale units ahead of low-SES children, a gap of nearly a year's worth of learning on the theta scale used by ECLS-K. But this large gap was entirely in place (0.64 units) at kindergarten entry and did not increase at all during the school years. It actually shrunk a bit![1] Once the dust cleared it turned out that the ECLS-K data revealed about the same story Heckman found. In fact, in the ECLS-K data, the *entire* eighth grade gap between high- and low-SES children in reading skills was in place by kindergarten and even narrowed somewhat by eighth grade. If we look at math gaps we find the same patterns.

Anyone who is seriously interested in how schools affect achievement gaps should take a long look at figure 2.1 and have questions. They should wonder whether this is just a weird pattern that happened to show up in Heckman's data and the ECLS-K but doesn't replicate in other datasets. The answer is no. Sean Reardon, an education scholar at Stanford, has also found that income achievement gaps are mostly flat across nearly every available longitudinal study including ECLS-K:1998 data (math and reading), Prospects (math and reading), Study of Early Child Care and Youth Development (math and reading), Longitudinal Study of American Youth (math and reading), National Education Longitudinal Study (math and reading), High School and Beyond (math and reading), and Education Longitudinal Study (math).[2] The patterns do not replicate precisely in all datasets but there is a dominant theme—achievement gaps increase very little during the school years.

And while achievement gaps merit attention, there is a more comprehensive way of conceptualizing inequality—How much variation in skills exists, and how does it change during the school years? Think of it this way: if a group of children take piano lessons from age five to eight we can look at how the gap in skills between high- and low-income children changes over the years (achievement gap approach) or we can measure how the variability in all children's skills changes between age five and eight (overall variation). While both approaches have value, this second tactic may provide a more complete perspective on how inequality changes.

Looking at *overall* variation in math and reading skills reveals that children vary considerably in skills when they arrive at kindergarten. The main question is: What happens to this variation after schooling begins? Does it increase during the school years, stay the same, or shrink? Figure 2.2 shows that, although reading skills improve over time, *variation* in reading skills, measured by the standard deviation (a measure of dispersion), declines over time. The standard deviation is 0.51 at kindergarten entry but just 0.39 in eighth grade. In other words, all children's skills became more similar over time. For math, we see roughly the same pattern, although the standard deviation doesn't change

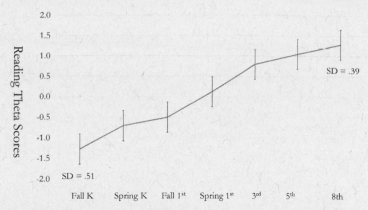

FIGURE 2.2. Variance in reading skills declines between kindergarten and eighth grade. ECLS-K:1998.

as much—declining from 0.47 at kindergarten entry to 0.45 in eighth grade (figure 2.3).[3]

So whether we look at inequality in terms of achievement gaps or overall variation, the patterns in figures 2.1–2.4 raise serious doubts about how much schools could possibly cause inequality in cognitive skills if inequality is already well-established before children start kindergarten. Of course, there is still the possibility that schools increase inequality somehow and that the patterns in the figures obscure important school processes, but in chapter 3 I'll show why that is unlikely.

Finally, there's another pattern that is troubling for the dominant narrative about schools. Not only are achievement gaps mostly formed at kindergarten entry, their trajectory changes once children start schooling (Figure 2.5). Prior to kindergarten, gaps between high- and low-SES children are growing rapidly. These gaps don't tend to grow much after schooling, however, and so there is a considerable difference between the magnitude of the gaps we observe among teenagers, and the gaps we would have expected to observe (dotted lines in figure 2.5) given their early childhood trajectories. This pattern suggests that schools are helping to reduce inequality.

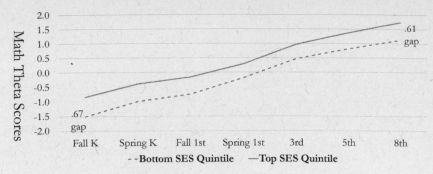

FIGURE 2.3. Socioeconomic gaps in math skills narrow between kindergarten and eighth grade. ECLS-K:1998.

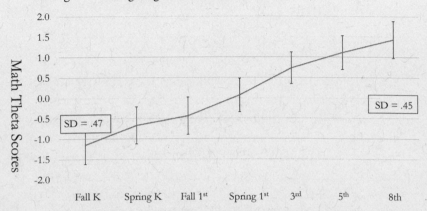

FIGURE 2.4. Variance in math skills declines between kindergarten and eighth grade. ECLS-K:1998.

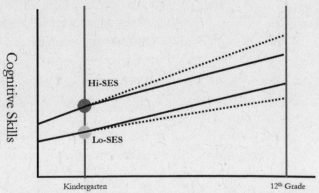

FIGURE 2.5. SES gaps in cognitive skills grow rapidly during childhood but then grow little during the school years (solid line). Had the gaps continued on the trajectory from early childhood (dotted lines), we would observe much larger SES gaps in twelfth grade.

SCALING MATTERS

It seems like every educational researcher interested in inequality should be shouting from the rooftops about the patterns in figures 2.1–2.4. One reason they don't is that the scholarly consensus used to be different. We used to think that achievement gaps grew quite a bit during the school years. For example, in the well-known Beginning School Study in Baltimore, gaps in unstandardized reading scores between poor and nonpoor children increased by a factor of nine between first and eighth grade—dramatically different patterns from the ones in figure 2.1. Studies like that led researchers to believe that targeting school reform was a good way to reduce gaps.

But the Baltimore study was almost certainly wrong on this issue. Since the 1980s, when the Baltimore data were collected, we've figured out how to measure children's skills better, especially how they change over time. To understand how we've improved the measurement of reading and math skills, consider a poor tape measure where the inches are not evenly spaced—the ones under three feet are much smaller than an inch and the ones above five feet are much larger than an inch. If we used this poor tape measure to estimate the difference in height between two children it would tend to underestimate the real difference when they are young and then overestimate it as they age. With this kind of measuring tape, it would be especially hard to know if gaps between two children grew over time.

This is the problem we had with the scales of math and reading used in studies like the Beginning School Study. They relied on a Thurstone scale, which turned out to be like a bad measuring tape. The Baltimore patterns likely underestimated the size of the gap at the beginning of school and then overestimated its growth during the school years because of several weaknesses in the Thurstone scales.[4] In contrast, modern psychometricians explicitly attempt to produce vertically equated scales via item-response theory (IRT), a measuring approach more adept at creating interval-level scales where each unit increase is similar, like each step up a staircase. In this way, increasing one point at the bottom of the scale is similar to increasing one point at the top. The gaps presented in figures 2.1–2.4 used IRT methods. There's just no way to know with certainty whether IRT scales succeed perfectly, but the newer scales are definitely closer to interval level than the older ones and provide a much better sense of how achievement gaps change as children progress through school.[5] Using the better scales may seem like a small technical issue but it ends up being a really big deal for education researchers because the better scales reveal that gaps are large at kindergarten entry and then change little during the school years, the pattern Heckman, Reardon, and I found. That has huge implications for how we might close gaps because it directs our attention more toward early childhood and less toward schools.

WHY THE EARLY YEARS ARE SO IMPORTANT

So now that we have better scales of children's cognitive skills and understand that most of the action shaping inequality occurs in early childhood, what are the early childhood conditions that produce such widely varying skills among children? Some would answer that it's simply a product of genetic variation. Some children are born smarter than others. While I do not dispute the position that meaningful genetic variation in cognitive skills exists, I note that the environment plays a powerful role. We can see that in two ways. First, achievement gaps in skills vary across time and place in ways that the genetic argument cannot readily explain. For example, Reardon found that the gap in reading in the U.S. between children at the top 10 percent versus bottom 10 percent in household income increased by 40 percent between the 1970s and mid-1990s.[6] It is highly unlikely that genetic changes in the population could account for that kind of increase in inequality of skills over such a short period of time. Second, there is also meaningful variation between countries in children's skills at the beginning of formal schooling. For example, Canada's children are several months ahead of American children in reading skills at kindergarten entry.[7] It seems unlikely, unless of course you're Canadian, that Canadian children are genetically superior to American children. It seems more likely that Canadian five-year-olds have better reading skills than American five-year-olds because they enjoy better environmental conditions, the result of several broader social policy decisions that Canadians have made differently than Americans. Notably, high-scoring Americans do about the same as high-scoring Canadians. It's at the bottom of the distribution where Canadian children really outperform Americans.

So how do environmental variations end up shaping children's early childhood development? The unfortunate news here is that some of what happens during the early years is hard to undo. Exposure to stress during early childhood changes physical aspects of the brain, which has consequences for the rest of the child's life. Robert Sopolsky, a Stanford neuroendocrinologist, describes how this happens. When children grow up in homes with frequent instability—food shortages, moving from home to home, different family members moving in and out—their brain develops differently. The stress of this kind of environment causes the size of the amygdala to increase and the prefrontal cortex to decrease, both of which are bad. The amygdala, the part of the brain that we share even with reptiles, is associated with our primitive emotions. A larger and more active amygdala results in a greater propensity toward anger and fear. Stress also reduces the development of the prefrontal cortex, the part of the brain that carefully weighs information, empathizes with others, and influences self-control.[8]

A 2015 study found that children exposed to poverty developed 8 to 10 percent less gray matter and scored four to seven points lower on standardized tests. About 20 percent of their deficit in test scores with other nonpoor children could be explained by maturational lags in the prefrontal and temporal lobes.[9]

In addition, when under stress the body produces glucocorticoids, a set of hormones that help us get fired up when we need to be, like when we need the adrenaline to run from a predator. It's really good that our body does this, but once the predator is gone it's a problem if we keep secreting high levels of glucocorticoids. Children who grow up in families with frequent stress tend to keep secreting glucocorticoids, even when they aren't necessary. This isn't good because when the brain is flooded with these hormones, it makes it more difficult for the child to sit still, focus on learning, and show empathy for others.

These unfortunate physical consequences of a stressful early childhood compromise the child's ability to succeed in school. Even a child with a strong desire to perform well will struggle due to an underdeveloped prefrontal cortex, oversized amygdala, and a brain flooded with too many glucocorticoids.[10] Unfortunately, stressful early childhood environments set children up for a lifetime of disadvantage. This evidence is consistent with an influential study from the National Research Council report, *Neurons to Neighborhoods*,[11] which concluded that challenging environmental conditions in childhood have epigenetic effects—they change physical aspects of the brain. The consequences of a challenging childhood, therefore, are significant. For example, one group of researchers found that among black children in Chicago, those living in severely disadvantaged neighborhoods suffered losses in cognitive skills that were similar to those from missing a year of schooling.[12]

This fact is not overturned by the observation that some children are resilient and overcome difficult circumstances. It is possible to find some children raised in highly stressful home environ-ments who perform better in school than some children raised in ideal home environments. But these exceptions do not contradict the rule but rather prove it by highlighting how rare they are. And of course, we don't know if resilient children would have turned out even better had they not endured early childhood stress.

RELATIVE DEPRIVATION MATTERS TOO

We might think that a good childhood is mostly about hav-ing reasonable material conditions, but families also become stressed as a result of their *relative* position in society. This hap-pens because we are social animals, shaped by a dominance hierarchy, and it is stressful for us to be on the bottom.

Being low on the totem pole among baboons is related to ex-cessive glucocorticoids, the stress hormone I talked about be-fore. Baboons on the bottom of the social hierarchy tend to have a sluggish glucocorticoid response to stress; that is, the response system doesn't increase as rapidly as it should, and then, once the stress is over, it stays at a relatively high baseline. The prob-lem for low-status baboons is too much glucocorticoid when nothing is going on and too little when they really need it. Hav-ing a system with too many glucocorticoids for most of the time is related to lots of physical problems like high blood pressure, low levels of "good" cholesterol, a poorer functioning immune system, and a higher frequency of getting sick.[13]

Of course, those are baboons and we're more interested in people, but we see similar evidence among humans. We know there is a strong link between someone's socioeconomic sta-tus (a measure of social rank) and their health. But interest-ingly, subjective SES measures (e.g., "In general, do you con-sider yourself lower class, working class, middle class?") predict health just as well as more objective measures (e.g., a composite of education, income, and occupational prestige). Similarly, independent of how much income families have, in communities where there is greater income inequality, there are also bigger gaps in health. This suggests that the problem is not just about being poor but also about *realizing* that you are poor.[14] Now, I'm not saying that two-year-old children have a good idea of their position in the stratification system, but their parents do, and knowing they are on the bottom adds to parental stress.

In addition, some goods are important because of their positional value. Earning a high school degree typically involves learning some market-based skills. But that's not its only value. It's also important because it provides you with a *relative advantage* in the job market over those without a degree. Once most people started earning high school degrees, however, then the competition moved on to college. In this way, one's *relative position* in the hierarchy matters. And even if the material conditions of the poor have been improving during the last century, and they have, we should still be concerned about the stress families endure when on the bottom of a hierarchy with little hope of moving up.

One problem in the U.S. is that the correlation between where one starts (what parents you are born to) and where one ends up is especially strong relative to other countries. We can see this by comparing how strong the influence of one's parents' starting position is on where the children end up. One way to do this is to compute the correlation between father's and son's income levels to assess how easy it is to rise above your parents' position. Ideally, we would not just restrict this to men, but that's the kind of data available across countries. To do this you pick an age for the father, say forty years old, and you note his income relative to everyone else his age. Then you wait until the son reaches that same age and you observe his relative income. The correlation between father's and son's income then represents the relationship between the two. Correlations range from -1.00 to 1.00, and a positive correlation suggests a link between where one starts and where one ends up. A correlation of 1.0 would mean that every son ends up in the exact same place his father did—rich kids are rich and poor kids are poor. A correlation of 0 would mean that where a son ends up has no relationship to where their father started. And a negative correlation here means that if a father was poor, it's more likely that the son will not be; that's not what we see in the U.S. or any country. So, the correlations are always positive, and the question is how strong they are. In the U.S. the correlation between father's and son's income is especially high, .46. In Denmark the correlation is just .16.[15] If your father is poor and you want to live the American Dream, you'd have a better chance in Denmark.

CONCLUSION

Knowing *when* achievement gaps emerge provides important clues about their causes. If schools played an important role shaping the gaps, then the gaps should grow quite a bit during the school years. Yet they don't. The fact that SES-based (and racial) gaps in reading and math skills emerge in force before children enter kindergarten should be the guiding mantra for policies aimed at reducing achievement gaps. It would be going too far to say that the inequality story is written in stone by kindergarten entry, but it's fair to say that it's a serious challenge to fix it after that age.

Scholars have known for some time that the first few years of life are important to childhood development, but they have put less emphasis on how these years are also the foundation of inequality. Early childhood plays a more important role shaping long-term inequality than we have appreciated. The big lesson from this chapter is that most of the inequalities in reading and math skills that we observe among teenagers were largely in place before kindergarten started. This has to make us question the role schools play in all of this. The answer, discussed in the next chapter, is a surprise to most.

CHAPTER 3

One Very Surprising Pattern about Schools

In addition to the fact that achievement gaps are primarily formed in early childhood, there is another reason to believe that schools are not as responsible for inequality as many think. It turns out that when children are in school during the nine-month academic year, achievement gaps are rather stable. Indeed, sometimes we even observe that socioeconomic gaps grow more slowly during school periods than during summers. That is not the pattern most social scientists would have predicted before collecting the data. If schools make inequality worse, then inequality should grow *faster* once kids are in school. Instead, the gaps don't change much or we even observe the opposite pattern — gaps growing faster when school is out.

Why isn't this pattern better known? Part of the problem is that most school data don't allow scholars to compare what happens when school is in (nine months) to what happens when school is out (summer). Most data are collected at just one point in time or, at best, annually. Only rarely have data been collected seasonally, at the beginnings and ends of each school year, allowing scholars to develop a better understanding of how schools matter.

So that leaves us with an important question—Which research should we trust? On the one hand are the patterns from traditional datasets suggesting that schools make inequality worse because correlations exist between low test scores and characteristics of schools serving disadvantaged children (e.g., large classrooms, inexperienced teachers, poor curriculums). On the other hand, there are the unique patterns from seasonal comparison studies, which are less numerous but suggest that schools are compensatory. I believe that the seasonal comparison studies, although smaller in number, provide a more accurate assessment of how schools matter than the larger group of traditional studies. Here's why.

SOCCER COACHES AND SCHOOLS

It's spring of 2003 and I just finished coaching my five-year-old son Nicholas's soccer game. We lost 9–0. The other team's players spent the afternoon taking shot after shot on our goal. After the game, as we walked toward the parking lot, I crossed paths with another dad and explained how we just got creamed. "It's all coaching," he said, grinning. We both laughed because he knew the players on both teams, and while coaching mattered, the kinds of kids you happened to get mattered a lot more.

The team that smoked us that day had several advantages. First of all, the teams in our league were constructed from both kindergarteners and first graders, but my team happened to have almost all kindergartners (twelve out of fourteen). In contrast, the other team had mostly first graders. You might not think that would matter much, but at that age one year of development is like 20 percent of the kid's life and it's a pretty big deal. Second, the other team had a pair of twins who were bigger, faster, and way better than everyone else. They scored nearly all of the goals. Just switch the twins to our side and we would have won the game. So, was I outcoached? Their team won 9–0 but it's hard to tell, given that the players we had to work with were so different.

One piece of information that would help us determine the best coach would be if we could somehow know how the two teams would have performed if the other coach and I had been switched at the beginning of the season—she coached my kids and I coached hers. That's what social scientists call the "counterfactual." It's a hypothetical, of course, because in reality we never get to know the counterfactual. But suppose we somehow were able to do this and my team (this time with the other kids) beat hers 5–0. If that happened, we would conclude that she really was a better coach than me because she won by more than I did when faced with the same challenge. Of course, we all know that a good coach of little kids doesn't run up the score but to simplify this discussion let's pretend that a better coach would win by more goals.

Like I said, we can't ever really know the counterfactual, and so social scientists have developed a tool they use for these kinds of problems: they statistically equalize two disparate groups in an effort to create an "apples to apples" comparison. This is what they are doing when they "control for" something like income differences between two groups, so that they can better understand how another variable, like education, matters. Essentially, they are finding people in their sample who have similar levels of income but still vary on education, and seeing whether there are still differences in outcomes. This strategy helps the social scientist understand what is going on, but the challenge here is that the two groups of soccer kids are *really* different. If you're thinking that this statistical adjustment would be hard to get right, you're correct. But it's often the only tool social scientists have for trying to create fair comparisons, and so they use it frequently.

Applying this imperfect tool to our question about soccer coaches would involve trying to equalize the kids on each team. To do this we would need to measure *everything* about the players that influences their soccer play—this might include the kids' ages, soccer experience, and speed. The social scientist then statistically "equalizes" the two groups of children on all of these characteristics and creates a new prediction for the outcome (game score) that assumes that all other conditions are now equal. If researchers did this for our two soccer teams, they probably would have identified how the other team enjoys older, more experienced, and faster players. Suppose that, after measuring these differences and making a statistical adjustment, the social scientists predict that the other team should have beaten us by seven goals. Then if we compare that prediction to what actually happened (we lost 9–0), we would conclude that, although the other coach was lucky to have better players, she was still better than me because her team beat us by a wider margin than what differences in our players' skills would predict.

Social scientists use this strategy all of the time, but I think I have a right to complain that it might not produce a fair comparison for me. Note how the social scientists identified *some* characteristics of the kids that they believed mattered—age, soccer experience, and speed—but for their statistical adjustment to work properly, two things have to happen, and these are both very challenging. First, they have to identify *everything* about the kids that matters to the outcome of the game, not just a few characteristics. For example, what if a kid's speed is meaningful, but their ability to control the ball and quickly change directions is more important? Or what if grit is really crucial? How willing is a kid to keep playing hard even when behind by a goal or two? (After we got down 3–0, one of my kids refused to play anymore. He ended up watching the rest of the game from the sideline while relaxing in a chaise lounge chair, drinking from his sippy cup.) If they miss any of these skills then the statistical adjustment will not be sufficient and the other coach will look better than she should.

And a second problem is just as important. They would have to measure children's characteristics perfectly. Suppose the researchers are persuaded that "grit" matters and then go on to measure it by how often the kid shows up to practice. That might be an easy way to measure it, but it also might be a really poor indicator. Indeed, for five-year-olds it's probably more indicative of the parents' schedules than the child's grit. The problem with this way of trying to create a fair comparison of the coaches is that, to successfully equalize the two groups of children, the researchers cannot miss any important skills or fail to measure them perfectly. And this problem becomes my problem because, to the extent that they fall short, they will almost certainly underestimate my coaching.

TRYING TO UNDERSTAND HOW SCHOOLS MATTER

So, let's get back to schools. The problem we ran into above, trying to determine how soccer coaches matter, is the same problem we have when trying to understand how schools promote learning. Children aren't randomly assigned to schools and so there are often big differences in the kinds of kids attending one school versus another. To isolate how schools matter, scholars might try to identify and measure lots of things that are different in children's homes and neighborhoods to make some sort of statistical adjustment, but they will struggle to identify everything that matters and then measure all of these characteristics perfectly. This is the problem the Coleman Report had, and it's the same problem most education research has had since. The statistical trick of "equalizing" two groups is well known to be insufficient. As a result, scholars who try to understand how schools matter with this traditional method will often misattribute differences in children's outcomes to schools because they did not sufficiently equalize the children's home environments (the eight-hundred-pound gorilla discussed in chapter 1). The problem is that when we use these traditional tools, schools serving disadvantaged kids almost always look bad, just like I looked like a bad soccer coach. This approach toward understanding schools is problematic because it stacks the deck against schools serving disadvantaged kids.

Let's consider how hard it is to statistically equalize children's home environments by identifying all of the characteristics about the home environment that influence children's development. Right away, there are a few things most of us would want to identify as important characteristics of the home—parents' income, education level, and occupation—the typical components of socioeconomic status. With a little more thought we might add family structure and stability, neighborhood quality, whether there are educational objects in the home (e.g., books, a computer), the frequency that parents read to the child, and whether the child is part of a historically disadvantaged racial group. With even more thought we might add indicators of things like how frequently the parents take the kid to the library or on vacations, and the quality of health care and nutrition. This sounds like a reasonable start, but it turns out that all of these kinds of measures explain only a fraction of why some kids learn faster than others. In a high-quality analysis of survey data, Burkam and colleagues tried to explain as much of the variation in children's summer learning as possible by including measures of socioeconomic status, race, family structure, gender, age, summer trips, summer activities, use of a computer, and whether the home language was English. This reasonably long list of covariates explained less than 15 percent of the variation in children's learning.[1] So, if 85 percent of why some children learn faster than others is unmeasured by these surveys, it's really hard for scholars to successfully identify and measure all of the characteristics needed to "equalize" children using statistical methods. The unobservable factors (unobserved because our surveys don't measure them) are just too big for this kind of problem.

Of course, this challenge is well known to social scientists, and so scholars have developed strategies for reducing its severity. One approach is to examine how much children learn, typically in a year, versus how much they know at one point in time. These "value-added" models are better because they do not reward or penalize a school for where children start, thus coming closer to identifying schools' real contribution to children's learning. This attractive feature is why many states now employ this method for evaluating schools. But value-added models, while a clear step in the right direction, still provide a distorted view of how schools matter because they assume that during the period of evaluation, typically one year, children go home to the same nonschool environments. That is not the case, however, and so value-added models still end up being biased against schools serving disadvantaged children. We know this, in part, because schools serving disadvantaged children look better if evaluated for gains during the nine-month school period than over a twelve-month calendar.[2] This is because schools are held accountable for what happens during the summer. Unfortunately for teachers and administrators working at these schools, almost all evaluations of schools are calculated using twelve-month data.

SEASONAL COMPARISONS

There is a better way to determine the best soccer coach. Suppose we have a good measure of the kids' soccer skills and we can gauge how much they improve when exposed to their soccer coach. This tactic is different than the one where we try and statistically equalize the children from the two different teams. Instead, we are trying to see how much kids' soccer skills improve when exposed to a coach. This is what is called an "exposure counterfactual" because it identifies how introduction to a particular condition matters. One advantage of this approach is that it does not require that we try to statistically equalize groups of different children, because each child serves as their own comparison. The question becomes, How much did children improve when exposed to my soccer coaching versus how much they improved when exposed to the other soccer coach?

Education scholars have applied this logic to schools, noting that the American school calendar, with its summer break, provides a natural experiment by allowing us to observe how things change when children are exposed to school versus not. For example, children's learning during the school year is a product of both school and nonschool factors, while children's learning during the summer is primarily a function of nonschool factors. The difference between the two, therefore, represents a good estimate of the school effect on learning.

The logic is similar to a crossover design in medical research, where patients are observed both on and off treatment. Researchers estimate the effect of a drug, for example, by observing how patients' outcomes change from a period of no drug treatment to a period of treatment. Similarly, researchers observe how achievement gaps change when children are on treatment (in school) versus not (summer). This way of estimating how schools matter doesn't require the questionable statistical manipulations of traditional techniques. Methodologists have praised the seasonal comparison strategy for identifying school effects because it provides a more compelling way of understanding how schools matter independently of children's home environments.[3] A big advantage to this approach is that it does not rely on our ability to statistically equalize highly disparate children.

There is another incredibly important advantage to seasonal comparisons. The overall consequence of all school mechanisms (both those that make inequality worse *and* those that reduce inequality) is observable in how inequality changes when school is in session versus out of session. This is especially important if past researchers have distorted our understanding of how schools matter by being more interested in finding school mechanisms that make inequality worse than in finding those that are compensatory. The advantage of the seasonal design is that it reveals the effects of *all* school mechanisms weighed against each other, regardless of any bias the researcher might have. Seasonal comparisons force a balanced account.

Seasonal comparisons also provide a broader lens on inequality than traditional methods. Consider the following scenario. Suppose we have a scale that ranges from −10 to 10 that gauges how schools affect inequality. A −10 indicates that schools reduce inequality substantially, zero means that schools are neutral, and a 10 indicates that schools make inequality much worse. Now suppose that the way the world really operates is that schools are a 2 and nonschool environments are a 7—both have characteristics that favor advantaged children but the nonschool environment is much worse for inequality. If the world operated this way, then schools would still be a compensatory institution. True, schools would still be advantaging the already advantaged, but not nearly so much as when children are out of school. The more children were exposed to school, therefore, the less inequality we would observe. This possibility is presented conceptually in figure 3.1, where I show how even unequal schools could be equalizing forces. One of the reasons this could happen is because the variation in children's nonschool environments is probably much greater than the variation in children's schools. There is good reason to believe that the world actually does operate this way (discussed in chapter 4).

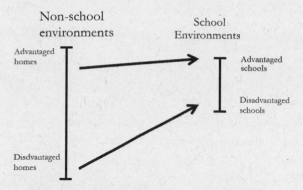

FIGURE 3.1. A contextual view: variation in non-school and school environments.

The problem with traditional scholarship on schools is that it lacks the perspective to describe this kind of world. Because it focuses narrowly on specific school processes (only the right side of figure 3.1), it lacks a broad enough lens to see how schools fit into the bigger picture. It's like trying to understand the success of a baseball team by focusing narrowly on how many errors are committed in the field. Yes, errors in the field matter, but they can be countered by runs scored while at bat. In contrast, seasonal comparisons take seriously the notion that children are shaped by both school and nonschool environments and that schools' effect on inequality is best understood within the broader social context.

Finally, unlike randomized experiments, which can be weak in generalizability, seasonal comparisons can be applied to nationally representative data, producing results that are reasonable for isolating how schools matter and more capable of describing the general patterns across the country. Of course, seasonal comparisons have their limitations (see appendix B) but these limitations are more modest than the sizeable ones that come from the traditional approach relying on statistically equalizing children.

WHAT DO WE LEARN FROM THE FEW STUDIES
THAT HAVE COLLECTED DATA SEASONALLY?

Analyzing schools from a seasonal perspective produces a very different understanding of how schools matter from what most people think. Some of the first seasonal studies were collected in cities such as New Haven, Atlanta, and Baltimore. Later, two nationally representative datasets, the Early Childhood Longitudinal Study—Kindergarten Cohorts of 1998 and 2010 provided the highest-quality seasonally collected data on children. The big question to ask from these studies is whether inequality grows faster when school is in versus out. The answer is that socioeconomic gaps in children's math and reading skills generally grow at the same speed when school is out (summer) versus in but when differences are observed, gaps usually grow faster when school is out; this is the dominant pattern in these studies. The combination of the summer and school year patterns implies that schools are largely neutral or even compensatory.

To understand the ramifications of this pattern, consider the conceptual drawing in figure 3.2. The figure visually displays the seasonal pattern we observed in our two studies of the ECLS-K datasets—gaps in skills between high- and low-socioeconomic status children hardly change during school periods but tend to grow somewhat during the summers. Now imagine what would happen if children did not attend school and the gaps diverged at the summer rate for the school periods too. The gap in skills would be larger. Schools appear to be doing something to quash the inequality that grows when school is not in session.

One lesson from all of this is that it prompts us to consider what we would expect inequality patterns to look like if children attended schools that were neutral. In that world I think it is reasonable to expect increasing SES-based achievement gaps. I say this because the nonschool factors that created large gaps

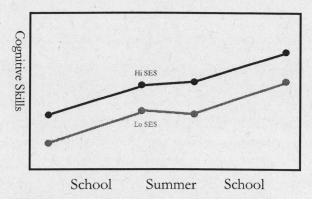

FIGURE 3.2. Gaps in cognitive skills are constant during school periods but grow during the summers.

at kindergarten entry should continue to matter once kids enter the school years. So even if schools had no effect on inequality, socioeconomic gaps in skills should continue to grow during the school years because of the continuing influence of children's disparate nonschool environments. Remember, children only spend a small fraction of their waking hours in school.

However, it's important to note that schools do not appear to be a "great" equalizer across all dimensions of inequality. For example, if we consider black/white gaps in skills, the seasonal patterns are messy and less encouraging. Heyns found evidence that the black/white gap narrowed more when school was in versus out in Atlanta during the 1970s,[4] but the Baltimore study in the 1980s was less clear. And our own work with the more recent nationally representative ECLS-K datasets finds little evidence that schools reduce black/white gaps, and occasional indications that schools make this gap worse, a pattern David Quinn, an education researcher at the University of Southern California, also reports.[5] Overall, some seasonal work has found that schooling reduces the black/white gap, some has been ambiguous, and some has found that schools increase the gap. The black/white gap, therefore, stands out as an exception to most seasonal patterns—there is at least some evidence that schools might be making this gap worse. That's why the subtitle of this book is about how The Assumption is *mostly* rather than entirely wrong.[6]

That said, there are two reasons why we should still continue to adjust our ideas toward a more positive view of schools than the one endorsed by The Assumption. First, schools appear to be compensatory in a broader way, and one that is more consistent with the socioeconomic than black/white patterns. We usually focus on achievement gaps between social groups (like high vs. low SES or black vs. white), but observing how the overall variation in skills changes may provide a more comprehensive understanding of the relationship between schools and inequality. I say this because it turns out that children's skills vary for many reasons unrelated to socioeconomic status or race/ethnicity. SES and race explain only one-quarter to one-third of the variance in children's test scores at one point in time, and only 1–9 percent of the variance in their learning rates.[7] Most of why some children learn faster (or slower) than others is unrelated to socioeconomic status and race, and so it's important to consider how exposure to school affects this bigger part (overall variance) of the inequality story. When we look at things in this big-picture way, we learn that exposure to school reduces overall variation in children's skills. Recall figure 2.2, showing that overall variation in children's reading skills declines between kindergarten and eighth grade (patterns for math are similar). That's a remarkable pattern that should immediately challenge notions that schools generate inequality.

We first pointed out this big overlooked part of the picture in our 2004 paper, "Are Schools the 'Great Equalizer'?," and we noted that variation in children's learning rates was two to three times greater in the summer than during the school years in the ECLS-K:1998 data. When kids were exposed to school they were much more likely to exhibit similar learning patterns than when they were not.[8] Importantly, our more recent work with the ECLS-K:2010 data replicates that finding.[9] This big-picture way of evaluating schools suggests that schools' overall effect mitigates inequality, a pattern more in line with the SES than the black/white pattern.

A second reason for rethinking The Assumption about schools and inequality, despite the black/white patterns, is that even though exposure to schools may increase black/white gaps, the magnitude of that effect is more modest than what most of us would have predicted. For example, in the ECLS-K:1998 data, the eighth grade black/white gap in reading is already 78 percent in place at kindergarten entry (94 percent in place for math).[10] So while the seasonal results hint that something about schools may be disadvantaging black children, they also highlight how most of the black/white gap can be traced to early childhood disadvantages. These numbers help provide some sense of proportion and they reveal that early childhood plays a bigger role (and schools a smaller one) than most people thought. The way to think about schools and black/white gaps is that schools might make them worse, but do not matter nearly as much as early childhood and probably less so than most of us would have predicted.

CONCLUSION

Maybe the coach of the soccer team that beat us 9–0 was better than me, but it's difficult to know because the children on that team were so different than the children on my team. It's also possible that, even though we lost badly, I was the better coach. Maybe if we had swapped players my team would have won 12–0. We never know these counterfactuals and the problem is hard to solve just by statistically equalizing the children on some list of characteristics we think are most critical to soccer. (This is why the film *It's a Wonderful Life* is so intriguing. Jimmy Stewart's character George Bailey gets to see the counterfactual world in which he was never born.) The statistical equalization improves the comparison, but falls far short of a fair comparison.

The surprising pattern about schools is that, when children are exposed to them, overall variation in skills and SES-based achievement gaps don't get worse. In fact, they sometimes decline. This pattern is at odds with The Assumption (that schools increase inequality) and scholars critical of schools have not offered a compelling explanation. Of course, the dominant narrative about schools has relied almost entirely on studies that try to understand how schools matter by statistically equalizing children's home and neighborhood environments. As I noted, this method probably distorts our understanding of how schools really matter because the statistical manipulation is usually insufficient. As a result, scholars typically overattribute differences in children's outcomes (like different reading skills) to school factors when they really stem from nonschool environments that were not completely "equalized." See appendix C for additional discussion regarding the challenges of understanding how schools matter.

Seasonal comparison studies use a more powerful research design. They do not rely on statistically equalizing children from different schools but rather follow the same children over time and ask how inequality changes when school is in versus out. This alternative approach provides a more compelling view of how schools really matter because it circumvents the problem most scholars face trying to "statistically equalize" groups of students attending different schools. It turns out that when you analyze schools with seasonal comparisons, you learn that they do more to reduce than increase most dimensions of inequality (with the notable exception of the black/white gap).

Of course, if the seasonal comparison evidence more accurately explains how schools matter, then this raises an obvious question: Why on earth does inequality not increase more when children are in school versus out? Surely advantaged children enjoy better learning environments in school than do disadvantaged children. The next chapter challenges that traditional view—The Assumption.

CHAPTER 4

And Now a Second, Even More Surprising Pattern

The unexpected news from the last chapter—that exposure to school doesn't seem to increase inequality along all dimensions—produces a puzzle: If disadvantaged children attend poorer schools, why don't SES-based achievement gaps increase when children are in school? It turns out that something we all *know* to be true—that schools serving high-income white kids are much better at promoting learning than schools serving low-income kids of color—may not be true after all.

SCHOOL ACHIEVEMENT, GROWTH, AND IMPACT

Consider the study I did with Paul von Hippel and Melanie Hughes entitled "Are 'Failing' Schools Really Failing?" We first evaluated the 287 schools in ECLS-K:1998 on the basis of their reading scores at the end of first grade.[1] We called this measure of school quality "achievement." You can see from figure 4.1 that the best schools had average reading scores in the upper 70s on this scale while the poorest schools had average reading scores in the bottom 40s. We identified the bottom quintile of schools as the ones most vulnerable to the "failing" label. These are designated with a dark dot in the figure to help us keep track of how these schools' relative position changes across evaluation

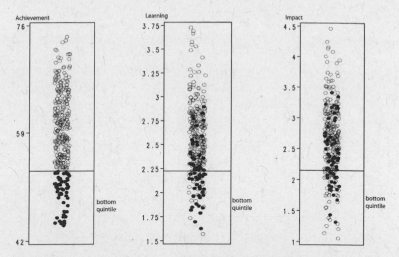

FIGURE 4.1. "Failing" schools identified by achievement (end of first grade score), growth (improvement from end of kindergarten to end of first grade), and impact (improvement in first grade learning versus summer learning). Evaluations of Schools, ECLS-K:1998. N = 287. (NOTE: Only the vertical positions are meaningful; points have been horizontally dithered to reduce overplotting.)

methods. Of course, defining the best schools this way (scores from one point in time) is clearly wrong because, as we learned in chapter 1, children arrive at kindergarten with very different skills and so most of the reason that one school has higher test scores than another has little to do with the school. It's kind of like comparing the records of two soccer coaches straight up, without recognizing that their players are very different. Really understanding the quality of what goes on inside the classroom requires isolating the contributions of the school from the child's family and other nonschool influences.

After constructing achievement measures, we evaluated schools with respect to how much children *increased* their reading skills between the end of kindergarten and the end of first grade—what we called "growth." The advantage of this measure is that schools are not rewarded or punished for the skills their children begin with but instead evaluated in terms of how much the students improve during a calendar year. Obviously, the growth model is a much better way to evaluate schools than the achievement measure. And this measure changes the perspective of which schools are doing well and which are doing poorly quite a bit. Note that in figure 4.1, quite a few of the dark-dot "failing" schools moved above the bottom quintile line. And a few of the schools scoring high on achievement have dropped below the line in terms of growth. The large difference in school "quality" between schools serving children from poor and non-poor families based on achievement is cut in about half when we emphasize growth.

While the growth model is a big step in the right direction, it is still not a fair, evaluative tool. It would be fair only if children from advantaged and disadvantaged families all went home to the same environments during the twelve-month period of study. Recall that the schools in our study were evaluated on gains children made between the end of kindergarten and first grade. We know, however, that during a calendar year, children spend the vast majority of their waking hours outside of school.[2] Some go home to stable family environments, where parents frequently ask them questions, provide carrots and hummus snacks, attend to children's medical needs immediately, help with homework, hug and kiss the child, and read them *Goodnight Moon* before bed. Others go home to unstable and stressful homes where a toothache goes unattended, an empty belly is not always filled, chaotic sleep patterns are the norm, and gunshots are a familiar sound. Schools have little control over the quality of children's home environments and yet the growth model holds them accountable for it. For teachers evaluated on the basis of how much their children learn, it is easier to look good when the children you teach go home to environments where the content is reinforced and the conditions support healthy development than if the children go home to environments that distract from learning.

So, if the achievement measure is bad and the growth measure still falls short, how can we evaluate schools in a fair way? To help explain our method, I want to briefly discuss what constitutes good evidence that one thing causes another. I'm not going to go back to the philosopher David Hume and debate whether we can ever identify causal relationships—my goal is more modest. I simply want to talk about the proper comparison when following subjects' outcomes over time and trying to understand if a particular event (or treatment) has a causal effect. And my discussion is restricted to a particular kind of study—the crossover design I mentioned earlier, where we observe how things change when subjects go from no treatment to treatment.

Suppose that we have a drug that we think might affect cognitive skills. To test its effectiveness, we give it to a group of subjects and follow them over time. And suppose that once the dust clears, we observe that the subjects' cognitive skills remained flat while on the drug (see figure 4.2). Should we conclude that the drug had no effect? If your answer is "not so fast," then you get points for already understanding the logical point I'm about to make.

To understand how the drug matters, we can't just observe the subjects' trajectory while on it; we need to *compare* that trajectory to when they were not yet taking the drug. The reason this is important is because our subjects might have been experiencing a rising trajectory in cognitive development before exposure to the drug (which would typically be the case, for example, if we were studying children). Observing no change in cognitive skills during the treatment period, therefore, would

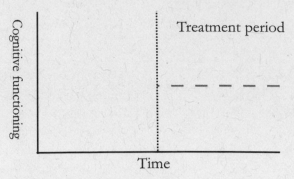

FIGURE 4.2. Does this drug affect cognitive functioning? We can't know until we see the patterns from the nontreatment (control period).

mean that the drug did matter (in a bad way) by reducing the gains we would have observed in its absence (denoted by the dotted line in figure 4.3). The dotted line is the "counterfactual" I mentioned before—what would have happened had the subjects not been exposed to the treatment. We never know for sure what the counterfactual path is (we can't observe it), but the dotted line is the most plausible estimate.

Thinking about testing the drug on a different group of subjects helps clarify why the comparison of the observed trajectory with the counterfactual one is so important. Imagine our subjects were elderly and experiencing cognitive decline prior to taking the drug (figure 4.4), but then that decline was arrested once exposed to the drug. We would now reach the exact opposite conclusion about the drug—now it's really good—than we did when studying children (figure 4.3). Note how in both cases the trajectory of cognitive skills while on the drug was the same, but our interpretation of how the drug matters is very different, depending on the trajectory the subjects were on prior to exposure. My point is that understanding how the drug affects cogni-

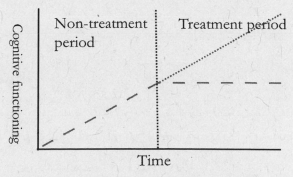

FIGURE 4.3. These patterns suggest that the drug has a negative effect on cognitive skills. The patients exhibit a flat trajectory while treated but they were gaining skills prior to treatment.

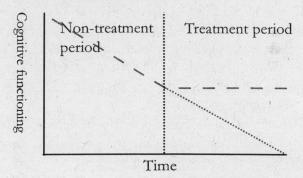

FIGURE 4.4. These patterns suggest that the drug has a positive effect on cognitive skills. The patients exhibit a flat trajectory while treated but they were losing skills prior to treatment.

tive skills requires comparing what happens during control and treatment periods.

When I'm in academic circles and I discuss the crossover design and causal relationships in these terms no one disagrees with me. They get it. But something weird happens when we transition to talking about schools. Some are prone to forgetting

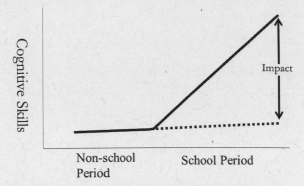

FIGURE 4.5. School impact: the difference in learning rates observed when children are exposed to school
versus not.

the logic behind crossover designs and want to identify school
effects by merely observing how children's outcomes change
when they're in school. But it's important to avoid looking to the
nine-month school period alone for our estimate of how schools
matter, even if it matches our intuition.

The importance of comparing treatment versus control periods is behind the logic that motivates the new measure of
school-based learning that my colleagues and I developed in
our "Are 'Failing' Schools Really Railing?" paper. First, we measured the rate at which a school's children learn when they're
not there, the summer before first grade (or nontreatment period), and then we compared this to how fast they learned once
in school (in first grade or treatment period). We described the
difference in these two rates as school "impact." Figure 4.5 displays the logic behind the school impact measure visually. The
key analytic leverage comes from observing how learning patterns change when children go from not attending to attending
school. We believe that this measure more accurately gauges the
quality of what occurs within the school walls because it cap-

tures how much things change once children are exposed to school.

It turns out that when we evaluate schools in terms of their impact, our ideas about which schools are performing well and which ones are not change in important ways. In our study, nearly three-quarters (74 percent) of the schools that were originally vulnerable to the "failing" label when gauged by achievement were no longer among the bottom-quintile performing schools when evaluated by impact. And interestingly, 17 percent of the schools that looked good via achievement were no longer rated highly via impact. These are schools that may boast high test scores but are probably not challenging their students sufficiently. If we are right and our impact measure more effectively captures learning attributable to schools, then we are currently underestimating the quality of schools serving disadvantaged children in a significant way. Existing evaluative tools based on achievement, and even growth, tend to conflate children's outcomes with their home environments.

Another way to see how our ideas of which schools are doing a good job change once we evaluate them fairly is to consider the correlates of school-based learning measures with school characteristics. If we stick with the achievement measure, then the traditional understanding of which schools are best is largely confirmed. Correlations reveal that schools with high achievement scores tend to have few children eligible for free lunch (poor kids) (−.38), or disadvantaged minority children (−.45), and are less likely to be public than private (−.44). These correlations are more modest if we evaluate schools by growth, however. The correlation between growth and disadvantaged minorities is smaller (−.28) and the correlations between growth and the percentage of children eligible for free lunch and public schools are no longer statistically significant. Finally, and most importantly, these school characteristics are all uncorrelated (none reach statistical significance) with the impact measure.

The impact results suggest that the distribution of school-based learning may be very different than what most of us assume. Yes, school-based learning varies across schools—some have very high impact and some have very little—but the schools with high-impact are no more likely to serve high- vs. low-SES children, or white vs. black children, or be private rather than public. School-based learning is distributed almost randomly across these social groups.

OBJECTIONS

Saying that schools serving disadvantaged children promote about the same amount of learning as schools serving advantaged kids is blasphemy in the academic world. I'd probably have more friends if I said that the earth is cooling. For this reason, it's worth considering several common objections.

(1) *It's easier to promote learning among children who start with weak skills.* Maybe schools serving advantaged children really do provide more school-based learning but it just doesn't show up on the impact measure because it's harder to produce learning among children who start with stronger skills. Don't we all make more progress learning some skill when we are trying to move from beginner to intermediate than when we are trying to move from intermediate to advanced? Think about how much more a kid improves during the first year of piano versus the fourth year.

This intuitive concern, however, is not a great explanation for the impact results for a couple of reasons. First, even if people gain skills faster when they are first learning a skill, we can create scales so that increases at the bottom represent about the same thing as increases at the top. Kids typically make more piano gains their first year than their fourth, but we can create a scale to reflect this. For example, at the bottom of the scale, a one-unit increase could represent the amount of progress kids typically make in their first year. Higher up on the scale, a one-unit increase could represent the gains children typically make in their fourth year. In this way, a one-unit increase at all ends of the scale means the same thing—the typical gains made by kids at that point on the scale.[3]

Second, even if it were easier to make gains when starting at the bottom of the scale, this weakness of the scale would apply to both school and nonschool periods. Seasonal comparison research depends on a comparison between seasons—school and summer—and so any weaknesses in the scale apply to both seasons. For this reason, the seasonal comparison research design makes it unlikely that scaling weaknesses explain the patterns.

Finally, some people mistakenly believe that it's too much to ask schools serving children with high skills to also produce high impact. This isn't a critique of the scale so much as just a complaint that it would be nearly impossible to be a high-impact school if you served kids from advantaged families. But that's not true. In our studies we have found that plenty of schools with high test scores (achievement) also manage to produce high levels of impact. For critics who worry that expecting high-impact from schools serving high-SES children is just too demanding, it may be that we are not expecting enough from some of the schools serving advantaged children. Perhaps if they were evaluated more fairly, via some kind of impact measure, schools serving advantaged children would be more motivated and we would see even more schools that produce both high achievement and impact.

(2) *No way would a high-SES kid learn just as much if they attended a school serving mostly low-SES children.* Many high-SES parents just know that the impact results are wrong because they think about it in personal terms. They are confident that

the school they have chosen for their child is a better learning environment because it has Advanced Placement French and provides violin lessons while the school serving mostly disadvantaged children does not. They think about how their own kid would lose these advantages in the school serving disadvantaged kids. They may be right about this. It may very well be that their own child would not learn as much if they attended the school serving mostly low-SES kids.

But note that what the impact studies are saying is different. They are finding that schools serving mostly disadvantaged children are doing about as well promoting learning in reading and math as schools serving mostly advantaged children. That doesn't mean that you could pluck a kid from the school serving advantaged kids and expect him to do just as well in the school serving disadvantaged kids. Schools probably specialize in meeting the needs of the children they typically serve. So, the value in the impact results is not so much in providing information about where parents should send their children, but rather in assessing how well schools are doing with the children they serve.[4]

(3) *Cognitive skills don't matter.* Even if convinced of the empirical patterns, some might argue that the impact results aren't that important because they only apply to cognitive skills like math and reading and that test scores don't matter much. I disagree. The stratification system in the U.S. has shifted toward a world where cognitive skills matter more now than they used to. That these skills are important is underscored by the associations between cognitive skills and a wide range of outcomes, such as early parenthood, dropping out of high school, incarceration, wages, and single parenthood. Higher levels of cognitive skills are consistently associated with better outcomes.[5]

The world wasn't always like this. In terms of the black/white gap, an important study using 1964 data found that black men with cognitive skills above the national average earned just 65 percent of what white men with similar cognitive skills earned, indicating that cognitive skills were not explaining much of the story of the black/white wage gap. Not even close. But then the world changed. For example, among employed men who were thirty-one to thirty-six years old in 1993, black men with test scores above the fiftieth percentile earned 96 percent of white men's average, indicating that, once cognitive skills were similar, earnings were almost similar. And when black and white individuals with similar cognitive skills are compared in more recent data, black individuals are *more* likely than white men to complete college. The role of cognitive skills has become increasingly important for understanding inequality. As Christopher Jencks and Meredith Phillips put it, "if racial equality is America's goal, reducing the black/white test score gap would probably do more to promote this goal than any other strategy that commands broad political support."[6]

(4) *School "quality" is about more than just promoting math and reading skills.* Even if persuaded that schools serving advantaged and disadvantaged children promote school-based math and reading learning at roughly similarly levels, and even if we were convinced that cognitive skills matter, most parents want more from a school than just these cognitive gains. They want their children's school to be a safe place with a positive atmosphere and culture. They want their child to have new and varied opportunities, like a chance to play soccer, join the chess club, and participate in the orchestra. And they want their children to attend a school with peers who are academically minded. That is part of why it's so important to distinguish between impact, which refers to school-based learning, and quality, which is a broader concept and encompasses much more.

The impact study does not demonstrate that there is no difference in the overall quality of schools serving advantaged and disadvantaged children because most of us define "quality" more broadly than just learning reading and math. It is almost certain that there are some advantages (beyond learning cognitive skills) to attending the schools serving mostly rich, white kids. Children come into contact with other people, both children and their parents, who have access to useful resources. For example, suppose your kid is not a great test taker but wants to go to a selective college. If they attend a school with advantaged children, they are more likely to be around peers who are talking about test preparation and perhaps taking a course to help them perform well on the SAT. They could even have a friend whose parent *teaches* the course and could provide additional insight into how to score well. They may also be advantaged by having a guidance counselor who has fostered relationships with elite colleges. In some cases, especially marginal ones, this counselor's support could be the difference.[7] And they obviously are more likely to be in classrooms filled with peers who have stronger academic skills and access to greater familial resources. These kinds of network connections are richer and more valuable in schools with advantaged students. And advantaged children tend to enjoy access to more experienced teachers.[8] This is partly because there is greater teacher turnover in schools serving disadvantaged children. In addition, advantaged children have more access to honors courses and Advanced Placement classes and a wider curriculum. These are all reasons why rich, white parents tend to want their kid to go to the school serving rich, white kids. Even though the parents are probably wrong about their kid learning more at this school, they're probably right about the kid enjoying other advantages.

But in the end what is amazing is that, despite all of these measurable inputs, advantaged children don't enjoy any more school-based learning than disadvantaged children. So while it is likely true that attending schools serving high-income children is advantageous in several ways, and parents may choose to send their children to these schools for these other reasons, these advantages don't seem to translate into better learning in the way we would expect. That's noteworthy, even if the schools do vary in quality in other ways.

In addition, although it seems reasonable that schools might promote inequality in ways other than learning math and reading, we probably should be less confident about this than we are. It's important to remember that before we evaluated schools fairly with respect to cognitive skills, we would have assuredly predicted that they produced more learning for children from advantaged than disadvantaged families. It's not until we more carefully isolate school from nonschool environments that we really get a sense of how schools matter. Unfortunately, we don't have that kind of information for very many outcomes beyond cognitive skills. In the few cases where we do, the results are in line with what we find for cognitive skills: schools play a more positive role than we thought. I talk about these in greater detail in chapter 6, but for now I'll just provide the punch line— schools seem to play a compensatory role influencing children's body mass index, and they play a neutral role with respect to their social/behavioral skills (e.g., paying attention, getting along with peers).

(5) *Schools serving advantaged children have the best teachers.* One thing has become clear in the last decade—some teachers are much better at promoting learning than others. Experimental studies (where children are randomly assigned to either teacher A or B) suggest that children improve 10 percentile points in a year when assigned a top- versus bottom-quartile teacher.[9] That children learn faster with some teachers than with others should not come as a surprise. We don't expect that all police officers are equally effective, or all dentists, or all NBA players. It would be weird to find no variation among teachers.

So, teachers vary in quality, but the problem is that this has led to a distorted understanding of how schools shape inequality. There is a mantra repeated by many education researchers that teacher quality is the most important school factor shaping learning. That appears to be true. But many come away from this research pattern thinking that, if teachers are the most important *school* factor shaping learning, the root source of inequality is poor teachers serving disadvantaged children. That's not the case and here's why. As we noted in chapter 1, gaps in children's skills are nearly entirely formed prior to formal schooling. The root source of inequality is disparities in early childhood environments.

And even when we restrict ourselves to looking at the little wiggles in achievement gaps during the school years, it's clear that variation in teacher quality is not a big factor in explaining these gaps. Stanford economist Raj Chetty and colleagues went to great lengths to develop a measure of teacher quality that is unbiased (i.e., captures teachers' actual performance rather than the kinds of students they teach). Once they produced a pretty good measure, they noted that it was virtually uncorrelated with students' family income, demonstrating that good teachers are everywhere. They wrote: "An auxiliary implication of these results is that differences in teacher quality are responsible for only a small share of the gap in achievement by family income. In the cross section, a $10,000 increase in parental income is associated with a 0.065 SD increase in eighth grade test scores (on average across math and English). Based on estimates of the persistence of teachers' impacts and the correlation between teacher VA [Value added] and parent income, we estimate that only 4 percent of the cross-sectional correlation between test scores and parent income in eighth grade can be attributed to differences in teacher VA from grades K–8. . . . This finding is consistent with evidence on the emergence of achievement gaps at very young ages (Fryer and Levitt 2004; Heckman, Stixrud, and Urzua 2006), which also suggests that existing achievement gaps are largely driven by factors other than teacher quality."[10]

Again, it should be emphasized that this does not mean that teachers do not matter. They matter a great deal. And getting a good one instead of a bad one matters a great deal for how much a child learns. But that doesn't mean that teacher quality explains *achievement gaps*. The reason is because teacher quality is distributed more evenly than we thought. It turns out that as we move toward measures that more fully account for children's nonschool environments, it is surprisingly difficult to make an evidence-based case that schools serving mostly high-income white children provide better learning opportunities—at least in reading and math—than schools serving low-income black children.

Finally, recall the patterns I presented in chapter 2—that SES-based achievement gaps sometimes grow faster when school is out versus in. That is a very difficult pattern to square with the position that advantaged children enjoy better teachers. If high-SES children do enjoy better teachers, then there must exist a wide range of other school factors countering that advantage in order to explain why SES-based gaps do not grow during school periods.

(6) *Do these patterns replicate?* With the release of the ECLS-K:2010 data, another nationally representative dataset with seasonally collected data, it became possible to assess whether the provocative patterns from our 2008 impact study could be replicated. David Quinn, Melissa Alcaraz, and I asked the same questions of the newer ECLS-K data: did schools serving mostly high-SES and white children produce similar levels of school-based learning compared to schools serving mostly low-SES and black children?[11] The answer is yes, the 2010 data produced the same patterns as the 1998 data. The newer 2010

ECLS-K data had some advantages too—we could observe impact across three years of schooling and two summers rather than one year of schooling and one summer (as we did in the 2008 study) and we were able to use a scale with a better claim to interval-level properties. So across two nationally representative datasets we observe the same patterns—very little difference in school-based learning (as measured by impact) between schools serving advantaged versus disadvantaged children.

(7) *The empirical patterns are restricted to kindergarten through second grade.* At present, the impact model has only been tested on young children, and we don't know if it would replicate among older children. Perhaps in the later grades we would start to see different patterns, with schools serving advantaged children producing substantially greater learning than schools serving disadvantaged children.

We don't know the answer to this concern right now, but what we do know suggests that the impact patterns observed among young children would likely extend into later grades. The reason I say this is because achievement gaps don't increase while children are in school (recall figure 2.1). That big-picture pattern matches well with the impact patterns from kindergarten through second grade and it would match well with data for later grades too. It would be surprising if the impact patterns changed much in the later grades, given how achievement gaps are so stable.

(8) *I don't believe the impact model.* Some might argue that there's just no way to separate school from nonschool influences—they are too intertwined. What happens at home affects a child's ability to learn in school, and what happens in school affects a child's home life. Schools, families, and neighborhoods are too intertwined for scholars to cleanly isolate how schools matter. I don't dispute that this is a challenge, but I posit that the impact model, through its emphasis on observing how

outcomes change when children are exposed to school versus not, addresses these concerns more successfully than traditional research (see appendix B for more discussion of the seasonal comparison method).

Nevertheless, some people just view the impact model as too novel and so may feel more comfortable assessing schools with more traditional value-added models. Importantly, even if we rely on value-added models rather than the impact measure, the literature would lead us to nearly the same conclusion. In addition to the Chetty study of teacher quality, a group of scholars from Mathematica asked "do low-income students have equal access to effective teachers?" and developed a value-added model (or growth model) to address the question.[12] The authors concluded that low-income children are, on average, exposed to teachers at the fiftieth percentile in the distribution while children from high-income families enjoy teachers only slightly better, from the fifty-first percentile. The difference is much smaller than most would think. The best read of the evidence, therefore, is that in carefully executed models that do a pretty good job isolating school effects, the difference in the opportunity to learn at school experienced by advantaged and disadvantaged children is either zero or very small. While I think the impact model provides the best way of assessing the quality of what occurs within the school walls, even if you are unpersuaded, the best growth models produce roughly the same conclusion—school-based learning is distributed almost evenly across advantaged and disadvantaged children.

CONCLUSION

Most of us would expect that schools serving advantaged children would promote much more learning than schools serving disadvantaged children. They certainly have higher test scores. But the even more surprising news from this chapter is that schools serving disadvantaged children produce about as much math and reading school-based learning as schools serving advantaged children. The traditional story is that low-SES children attend dramatically poorer schools and, as a result, are far behind their high-SES peers. It is probably more accurate to say that low-SES children arrive at kindergarten far behind but then mostly stop losing ground once in school.

We know less about which schools are good at promoting learning than we think. I watched my two kids go through our local school district in Mount Vernon, Ohio. I met frequently with their teachers, was often inside their classrooms, and had personal relationships with many of the teachers and administrators, and yet I would not even have a reasonable guess as to whether their school was above or below average in terms of school-based learning. Although we talk confidently about "good" and "bad" schools in our local areas, most of us have little idea where our schools would rank in terms of impact. If you think about it this should not be too surprising. To really understand the quality of what occurs within a classroom would require extensive observation and in-depth knowledge of best practices, way more information than most of us have.

For advocates of market-based school reform, the implications are dire. The argument for market-based school mechanisms is that choice allows parents to pressure school systems by voting with their feet, which then provides the proper incentive for school administrators and teachers to produce more learning. But this view of school reform depends on parents having access to good information about school quality in order to make good choices. Impact studies suggest that achievement and even growth model information are poor indicators of school quality. Parents relying on that kind of information would often go in the wrong direction, pulling children out of pretty good schools and sometimes sending them to pretty poor ones. With such poor information, some market reforms are likely inefficient, perhaps so much so that they even work in the wrong direction, rewarding bad schools and punishing good ones. And unfortunately, these market-based reforms can lead to greater segregation based on race and income.[13] When deciding on a school, parents don't analyze a school's reading and math scores and then attempt to isolate the school effect via an impact model. Instead they ask relatives, friends, and co-workers about the best schools, a dynamic that likely promotes the concentration of advantaged kids in the same schools, regardless of quality.

Note that this is very different from saying that there are no terrible schools serving disadvantaged children. Figure 4.1 reveals that some of the "failing" schools on the basis of achievement are also "failing" on growth and impact. So, if the question is whether terrible schools serving disadvantaged children exist, the answer is yes. But the question should be, on average do the schools serving advantaged children promote more learning than the schools serving disadvantaged children? Here the answer is no because, once evaluated fairly, there are many more schools serving disadvantaged children that are doing better than we thought and many more schools serving advantaged children doing less well than we thought. This pattern is only revealed, however, when we develop a measure of schools that no longer rewards or punishes the school simply for the kinds of children it happens to serve.

When we recall that schools serving disadvantaged children are achieving similar learning rates despite the challenges that disadvantaged children face at home, it could be argued that schools are doing even *more* for disadvantaged than advantaged children. The idea that schools reduce inequality may seem improbable but we haven't thought enough about schools' compensatory practices. The problem is that we continue to blame schools because the dominant narrative matches our gut feeling about schools. But given how our gut feeling about schools and inequality is contradicted by critical evidence, perhaps we should think about this whole thing differently, the goal of part 2.

Part II

A NEW WAY TO THINK
ABOUT SCHOOLS AND
INEQUALITY

The big problem with The Assumption—*children learn more in schools serving high-income and white children than in schools serving low-income and minority children*—is that it doesn't fit the patterns that I described in chapters 1–4. Of course, some patterns for the black/white gap point to schools as a culprit, but it is not enough to overcome the larger story. Sometimes empirical patterns suggest a minor tweak in our thinking while at other times they are fundamentally at odds with traditional thought. This is a case of the latter. The patterns from part 1 are more than just annoying for the prevailing narrative about schools and inequality; they suggest that we need a fundamentally new view.

The 1966 Coleman Report's controversial claim was that schools were mostly neutral when it comes to explaining gaps in children's cognitive skills. The report famously concluded: "One implication stands out above all: That schools bring little influence to bear on a child's achievement that is independent of his background and general social context; and that this very lack of an independent effect means that the inequalities imposed on children by their home, neighborhood, and peer environment are carried along to become the inequalities with which they confront adult life at the end of school."[1]

Coleman used the best social science techniques at the time, but we now have better ways to analyze data. Critics have pointed out how he relied on correlations observed at one point in time and how he was unable to parse out within- versus between-school factors at stake. In short, the Coleman Report was based on analyses with significant limitations. So if Coleman's study was imperfect, then maybe schools influence inequality much more than he claimed.

Coleman's study *was* flawed, but it turns out that the overall conclusion was still mostly right. Indeed, to the extent Coleman got it wrong, he failed to appreciate fully schools' compensatory role (described in chapter 6). When we use more modern methods, we don't end up concluding that schools play a larger role exacerbating inequality than Coleman thought; we end up concluding that schools play a more compensatory role than he appreciated.[2] When it comes to inequality, schools aren't worse than Coleman thought, they're better.

So how *should* we think about schools and inequality? I argue that we should think of them more like reflectors than generators of inequality (chapter 5) and as more compensatory than exacerbatory (chapter 6). My main message is that schools play a different role with respect to inequality than we thought, especially with regard to cognitive skills. Developing an accurate understanding of how schools matter is important because it shapes the kinds of efforts that are most effective at reducing inequality. For this reason, I consider why we cling to The Assumption (chapter 7) and articulate how this mistake is costly (chapter 8).

CHAPTER 5

More Like Reflectors than Generators

Schools are more the place where we observe inequalities and less the place where they are produced. They reflect more than generate inequality.

My position in this chapter, however, needs to be understood as proportionate—schools *mostly* reflect rather than generate inequality in cognitive skills. That means that some school characteristics do generate inequality. Schools are not entirely passive and in this section I briefly discuss some of the school mechanisms that likely increase inequality and undergird the dominant view of schools. My main point is that these school mechanisms can all exist, and yet The Assumption can still be wrong for two reasons. First, these exacerbatory school mechanisms, once carefully analyzed, tend to play a more modest role in influencing achievement gaps than previously thought. Second, even when they do make inequality worse, exacerbatory mechanisms are outweighed by compensatory mechanisms that are often overlooked.

SCHOOLS GENERATING INEQUALITY

There are several characteristics of American schools that likely increase inequality. For example, whenever local tax bases play a significant role in school funding, school districts located in wealthy areas enjoy more revenue than school districts located in poor areas. Because some states continue to rely heavily on local taxes, there remain differences in resources between schools serving disadvantaged and advantaged children. In some cases, these differences are considerable. In addition, many teachers acknowledge that their first choice is not to work at a school serving disadvantaged children, and so it would seem that these schools would struggle to attract and retain good teachers. In addition, peer composition likely shapes how much a child learns. Sitting next to college-bound peers probably contributes to the learning environment.

Another way in which schools may increase inequality is via the curriculum they provide. Schools serving disadvantaged children often promote plug-and-chug rote memory skills while schools serving advantaged children more frequently emphasize advanced skills like synthesis, evaluation, creativity, and leadership. In this way, the economists Samuel Bowles and Herbert Gintis argue, the school system prepares disadvantaged children to be obedient workers in working-class jobs while it prepares advantaged students to be managers. Jean Anyon builds on this argument, noting that in schools serving elite students there is a sense that students themselves can produce knowledge, while in schools serving working-class children knowledge is understood as something imposed on them by others.[1]

There is also good reason to believe that black and low-SES children are sometimes treated less well in school than their advantaged counterparts. One argument is that teachers are mostly white and come primarily from the middle class and so their behavioral expectations do not always align with the behaviors exhibited by disadvantaged students. As a result, teachers are often too quick to define a student from a disadvantaged background as disobedient because the child's behavior does not match their expectations. To the extent that these cultural mismatches are less about disadvantaged students' misbehavior and more about the way teachers define children's behavior, this is an example of a school mechanism that contributes to inequality. As one example of this problem, a study of children in the Tennessee STAR experiment found that black students randomly assigned to a black teacher between kindergarten and third grade were 7 percent more likely to graduate from high school and 13 percent more likely to enroll in college than their counterparts who were not assigned a black teacher.[2]

There are other reasons to suspect that minority and low-SES children are treated unfairly in the school system: they are more often identified as learning disabled and they are more frequently disciplined than other students. In addition, they are underrepresented in high-ability groups and honors and AP classes. Of course, the extent to which schools generate rather than reflect these patterns is not entirely clear. For example, low-SES boys will be disciplined more than other groups if they misbehave more, but some scholars argue that schools disproportionately punish low-SES boys above and beyond their actual behavior.[3]

Perhaps the school characteristic that receives the most attention, however, is teacher quality. Good schools enjoy better teachers than bad schools, the argument goes, for several reasons. Teaching at a school serving disadvantaged children is more challenging than teaching at a school serving advantaged children. For example, disadvantaged children start with lower skills, have more behavioral and health problems, are more frequently absent, more often change schools in the middle of the year, and receive less support at home. Teaching disadvantaged children is harder, and so the best teachers migrate to schools serving advantaged children. In contrast, the poorest teachers end up at schools serving disadvantaged children. The documentary *Waiting for Superman* describes a process called the "dance of the lemons," where poor-performing teachers are traded around among principals serving disadvantaged children.

So, given all of these ways in which schools' characteristics and processes might make inequality worse, how can the dominant narrative be misplaced? One reason is that many of the school characteristics thought to exacerbate inequality have more modest consequences for learning than we thought. Let's consider three that have received a lot of attention: financial resources, teacher quality, and ability grouping.

It turns out that since the *Serrano v. Priest* rulings in the 1970s, school funding in the U.S. has become more equal than most people realize. If I ask my undergraduate students at Ohio State to estimate how much more school districts serving high-income children spend versus school districts serving low-income children, they guess that the schools serving high-income children spend two or three times as much as the schools serving low-income children. The real difference is much smaller. In Ohio, districts serving high-income children (the top quartile of schools) spent an average of $11,892 per child in 2012 compared to $10,293 in districts serving low-income children (the bottom quartile of schools)—just 13.4% more money for the schools serving advantaged kids. Is Ohio unusually egalitarian? No, in fact it's one of the more unequal states in the country. The average difference, surprisingly, between per pupil expenditures among schools serving mostly high- versus mostly low-income students in the U.S was $193 dollars per pupil in 2012 (1.7 percent). In the majority of states, school funding formulas actually direct more money to districts serving poor rather than rich kids.[4]

I know this information feels wrong. It sure seems like schools serving advantaged children have way more money than those serving disadvantaged children. And sometimes the story does fall the way we expect. For example, in the Columbus area, most people would list Bexley, Upper Arlington, and Worthington as among the best school districts while putting the Columbus city school district near the bottom. So how much money does each district spend per pupil? We see the expected pattern when comparing the Upper Arlington and Columbus city school districts—Upper Arlington spends more. But even here the difference is smaller than most expect—$15,157 in Upper Arlington versus $14,613/child in Columbus during the 2011– 12 school year. And the Bexley ($14,348/child) and Worthington ($13,367) districts actually spend less than the Columbus city school district.[5]

Of course, per pupil expenditures aren't the perfect indicator of resources. Even if funding is equal, for example, there might be less money for instruction for students attending an old building that is expensive to maintain.[6] Or districts with wealthy parents may enjoy substantial additional funds from successful Parent Teacher Organization fundraising attempts, a much weaker source of revenue for schools serving low-income children. Nevertheless, overall differences in school funding are smaller than most people think.

Now let's consider how big a role teacher quality plays in shaping inequality. Teacher quality is widely thought to be the school characteristic with the largest influence on children's learning. It is true that children attending schools serving mostly advantaged children have much higher math and reading scores than children attending schools serving disadvantaged children, but it turns out that very little of this has to do with differences in the quality of teachers.

To repeat the lessons from chapters 1–4, most of the SES achievement gaps are formed prior to kindergarten and then, once in school, advantaged and disadvantaged children learn at roughly similar rates when school is in session. And the scholars that have tried to carefully isolate teacher quality, like the Isenberg et al. and Chetty et al. studies described earlier, reveal that differences in quality (defined as promoting learning) between teachers serving advantaged and disadvantaged children are very small. Recall that Isenberg and colleagues concluded that advantaged children enjoy teachers just one percentile better than disadvantaged children. And Chetty and colleagues concluded that just 4 percent of eighth-grade income-based gaps in skills could be attributed to variations in teacher quality.[7] My own work (described in chapter 4) suggests that schools serving advantaged and disadvantaged children produce the same amount of school-based learning (impact). While it is true that teachers vary in quality in meaningful ways, it turns out that there are good and bad teachers across schools serving advantaged and disadvantaged children and that the distribution of good teachers is more even than we thought.

Finally, scholars originally thought that the practice of ability grouping played an important role exacerbating inequality because advantaged children were unfairly assigned to higher groups and then enjoyed better instruction. But on closer inspection, the degree to which group assignments promote inequality is less clear. Yes, some studies find that even when children have similar reading test scores, high-SES children are more likely to be assigned to a higher reading group, but it's unclear that this is a discriminatory process because the reading test score does not perfectly gauge children's skills. The teacher may have additional information, potentially unbiased, that merits the allocations. In addition, children assigned to high-ability groups sometimes learn more during a year than children assigned to low-ability groups. This could be evidence of a pernicious school process, but it might also reflect differences in the children's nonschool environments, which continue to vary during the nine-month school year and during the three-month summer.

Perhaps the biggest reason, however, that these school processes (i.e., funding, teacher quality, ability grouping) don't
necessarily result in greater inequality is because even if they do
end up making inequality worse, they are only one-half of the
story. There also exist school processes that reduce inequality.
We hear less about these, however, and so I'll discuss compensatory school processes in more detail in chapter 6.

TWO EXAMPLES OF SCHOOLS REFLECTING
BROADER SOCIETY

In contrast to viewing schools as generators of inequality, we
can look at them as reflecting inequalities that have nonschool
origins. The way that schools reflect broader society is supported by two examples, one cross-cultural and one historical.
First, the cross-cultural example. Joseph Merry, an assistant
professor of sociology at Furman University, documented that
Canadian children are ahead of U.S. children by a sizeable 0.30
standard deviation units (nearly a year's worth of learning) in
the Programme for International Student Assessment (PISA)
reading test given to fifteen- to sixteen-year-olds.[8] But the bril-
liant insight from Merry's study was to assess the magnitude of
international gaps in skills before children start formal schooling. Merry also compared similar-cohort Canadian and U.S.
children on the Peabody Picture Vocabulary Test (PPVT) reading test at ages four to five, before formal schooling had started,
and found that a similar gap of 0.31 standard deviation units was
already in place at that age.

To understand why American four- to five-year-olds are so
far behind Canadian four- to five-year-olds in vocabulary skills,
Dan Zuberi's study reveals how much harder it is to be poor in
the U.S than in Canada.[9] Zuberi compared hotel workers in Vancouver with those in Seattle. Both worked for the same large
hotel chain; the main difference was just that one group lived
in Canada and the other in the U.S. Zuberi showed that these

mostly entry-level and minimum-wage workers (housekeeping, laundry staff, doormen, bartenders) were better off in Vancouver for a variety of reasons. First, the workers in Canada were more likely to have union representation. Union strength was about the same in the two countries after World War II, but then it declined in the U.S while it did not in Canada. Even though Washington State is considered labor friendly, the percentage of unionized workers is only 18 percent compared to 30 in Canada. Zuberi argues that the higher rate of unionization is not a function of different preferences (Americans are actually more supportive of unions than Canadians). Instead, he argues that it is a result of policy differences. Specifically, the American system requires a long and protracted campaign prior to a union vote. During that time, management can thwart union efforts via delay and discriminate against union leaders and supporters. In contrast, union formation in Canada is more straightforward, minimizing the opportunity to resist unions. The consequences of different levels of unionization are nontrivial. Unionization results in better wages, working conditions, and job security for Canadians than Americans.

And Canadians enjoy universal health care while about 15 percent of Americans lack any kind of access to health care. This means many Americans don't use preventive care (e.g., screening, yearly checkups), which increases vulnerability to long-term problems. Ultimately, forgoing preventive care is usually more expensive. In the U.S., the hotels provided workers with health care, but there was a probationary period of six months. In practice, this meant that about one-fourth of the U.S workers Zuberi studied lacked health insurance. In sum, due to policy differences, Canadian children enjoy more favorable early childhood environments than American children and show up to kindergarten better prepared.

Second, historically we can see evidence that achievement gaps in the U.S. have changed over time. We know that the black/white achievement gap declined by about one-third during the 1980s, a change scholars attribute in part to the increasing education of black parents. And as mentioned in chapter 2, Reardon found that the gap in reading in the U.S. between children from the top 10 percent and bottom 10 percent (in terms of family income) increased by about 40 percent between the 1970s and mid-1990s.[10] Of course, it might have increased because of changes to schools. Schools did change during this period in meaningful ways, becoming more focused on testing, accountability, and parental choice. Scholars have noted that the expansion of charter schools and school choice has been related to increased racial segregation.[11] Perhaps these same mechanisms resulted in greater school-based inequality, which led to growing achievement gaps. But Reardon explores the more obvious explanation, growing income inequality in households. He concludes that growing income inequality may not have been the only factor at stake, but that the link between income and cognitive performance increased over time. In other words, poor children have always performed below rich children, but over time this difference has grown and the correlation between income and math and reading skills has become stronger. The main point is that the outside-of-school context changed over time and subsequently the achievement gaps observed in schools grew. Cross-national and historical comparisons highlight how patterns that we might be tempted to attribute to schools are actually products of larger social phenomena.

WHAT ABOUT THOSE HIGH-FLYING SCHOOLS?

But schools that serve disadvantaged kids and improve their math and reading scores significantly do exist. What about those? Don't they prove that school reform itself can address achievement gaps? Don't they show that schools can do more than reflect, that they can play a powerful role changing inequality?

The first thing to note about high-flying schools (high-performing schools serving disadvantaged children) is that there ends up being fewer of them than we would like. We often see reports identifying high-flying schools and then, once we look closer, we learn that they were only medium-flying or even low-flying or sometimes not flying at all. A high-flying school is typically identified as producing better-than-expected test scores given the population of students it serves. A school might be identified as high-flying, for example, if it produces strong math scores among fourth graders. The problem is that scores bounce around a bit, even average scores for schools, and so sometimes a school looks pretty good for one grade of students on a single outcome for reasons that are hard to explain. Maybe they happened to have a few fourth graders who were really good at math that year. Or maybe a teacher did a good job preparing students for that particular test. Or maybe the fourth graders guessed well on the test. We're not sure.

But if the school is really terrific, then the good news shouldn't be restricted to fourth grade, or to math scores, or to a single year. We should observe better-than-expected performance on a consistent basis. When we require more comprehensive and consistent evidence of high-flying, then the number of impressive schools serving disadvantaged children goes way down. Rothstein started with a long list of allegedly high-flying schools but ended up with only a small handful that were really doing better than expected with disadvantaged children on a consistent basis.[12]

And even among this group there is a disconcerting percentage that are fraudulent. For example, in Louisiana, T. M. Landry School gained a reputation for taking underprivileged black students and getting them into elite colleges. They were so successful that they started making videos of their students receiving their college acceptance information. One video of a student learning of his acceptance to Harvard has been viewed more than eight million times on YouTube. Unfortunately, the school was involved in widespread fraud, creating fake essays that exaggerated the barriers the students faced growing up, and creating fraudulent transcripts of classes the students never took. The fairy tale story just wasn't true for most students, many of whom described abuse at the school.[13]

Of course, there still are a handful of schools that actually do a better-than-expected job with disadvantaged children—real high-flying schools. The most persuasive evidence comes from experimental studies where children are randomly assigned to either attend a treatment school (usually with some meaningful reforms) or a traditional public school. This kind of study is powerful because we can be reasonably confident that the two groups of students—the ones attending the treatment school and the ones attending the public school—are equal in all ways beyond just rough demographics.

Although their numbers are small, these high-flying schools merit attention. As one example, children randomly assigned to schools employing comprehensive reform, such as those in the Harlem Children's Zone,[14] Knowledge Is Power Program (KIPP), and the effective reforms employed by the University of Chicago Charter School,[15] learned more than children who attended traditional public schools. Similarly, the authors of *The Ambitious Elementary School* describe school reforms (e.g., increased school exposure, greater sharing of information across teachers and staff) that reduced black/white gaps among children in Chicago public schools by nearly two-thirds.[16] And the Boston preschools employing the *Opening the World of Learning* (OWL) literature program closed the black/white gap by one-third.[17] These random-assignment studies represent the most powerful evidence that schools actually can reduce achievement gaps. Clearly schools *can* play a meaningful role reducing some aspects of inequality.

For some, the fact that any high-flying school exists means that we should identify the school mechanisms that work in these small studies and scale them up to a societal level. If school reform can significantly improve the performance of disadvantaged children in small-scale studies, imagine what it can do for everyone.

This scaling-up approach to school reform may work in terms of raising the overall learning among American students, but it's not a great approach for reducing inequality. High-flying schools are terrific and I wish there were more of them, but they are a suboptimal means for reducing societal-level inequality primarily because the gaps are already well formed before kindergarten entry and so they are necessarily remedial. My main point is not so much that school reform can't help but that it's unlikely to be the most efficient way to reduce inequality. Instead, we would be better off addressing the large inequalities in children's early childhood environments and preventing large achievement gaps from emerging in the first place.

There is a second problem, a political challenge, to the school-based approach to reducing inequality that I will discuss in more detail in the final chapter. Briefly, when we find evidence of schools' promise in reducing inequality from current small-scale studies, it's always a result of interventions where disadvantaged children have received a better school treatment while advantaged children do not receive the treatment. I know of no study where both advantaged and disadvantaged children were exposed to better school treatments and achievement gaps declined in the same way that they decline when the disadvantaged children alone receive the treatment. Scaling up school reforms to the societal level as a means for reducing SES-based achievement gaps, therefore, would produce similar effectiveness only if the reforms were available to disadvantaged children and denied to the advantaged.

UNDERESTIMATING EARLY CHILDHOOD

Part of why we need to think of schools more as reflectors than generators of inequality is because early childhood plays a more central role in shaping children's trajectories than is typically appreciated. Social scientists have been talking about the importance of early childhood for years, but for some reason when it comes to understanding achievement gaps, they continue to underestimate its importance.

There are lots of reasons to believe that it is less expensive to improve children's lives early on than to wait and address problems later in life. Heckman and Masterov describe a few ways to do this that are not necessarily cheap but end up being cost effective in the long run.[18] For example, in one of the most famous examples, the Perry Preschool program, a group of children were randomly assigned to either receive high-quality preschool for two years (and weekly home visits with parents) or not. By age twenty-seven, the treatment group averaged 2.3 arrests compared to 4.6 for the control group. In a similar study at Syracuse University, only 6 percent of children exposed to high-quality day care for a year had probation files later in life, compared to 22 percent of the control group.

Of course, these kinds of high-quality preschool programs cost money. The Perry Preschool program cost $19,162/year per child, and the Syracuse University program cost $54,483/year per child in 2004 dollars. The costs up front are hefty, but the payoffs in the end are also substantial because of the savings from more time working and paying taxes and less time in prison and on welfare.[19]

I think Heckman and Masterov are right, that investments in early childhood are the way to go, but while high-quality preschools might be a good investment, there may be an even better way. Preschool programs typically start at age three or four and probably come too late to have the optimal impact because there is reason to believe that achievement gaps are mostly formed by age three.[20]

Trying to help disadvantaged children via expanded preschool programs may be less effective than simply improving their lives directly via cash transfers. The economist Grover Whitehurst compared the bang-for-the-buck observed in several preschool programs versus the Earned Income Tax Credit (EITC), which gives low wage earners more money through a tax benefit. It turned out that for every $1,000 spent per child, the EITC raised reading skills 0.06–0.08 standard deviation units while the preschool programs only raised skills 0.01–0.02. Both kinds of programs helped, but the EITC helped more.[21] It may be that reducing the financial stress in homes that endure poverty is the single most effective way to improve the learning environment for disadvantaged children. So while Heckman has been a prominent advocate of early childhood investments, it's not clear that his avenue for doing so (preschools) is optimal.

It remains unclear what kinds of early investments are most effective, but the bigger policy lesson is clear—our policies should be shaped by the fact that early investments reap the most benefits. Part of the reason early investments matter the most is that, as Heckman puts it, "skills beget skills"—early skills are often prerequisites for more complex skills. Understanding addition is necessary before multiplication makes sense. Get on the wrong track early and the children are playing catch-up for the rest of their lives, and so it is best to confront gaps early.

CONCLUSION: A DIMINISHED ROLE FOR SCHOOLS, AN ENHANCED ROLE FOR EARLY CHILDHOOD

To understand schools accurately it is important to recognize that they exist within a broader context. If that broader context is highly unequal, it is likely that we will observe large inequalities in schools. And it is easy to confuse the inequalities we observe in schools (like achievement gaps) as a product of the schools themselves when they really are due to the unequal social environments in which those schools exist. This contextual view of schools is usually not obvious to us, but it can be readily understood by comparing achievement gaps across countries or observing how they change over time.

When it comes to understanding inequality, schools play a smaller role than most people think. Achievement gaps are formed much more by inequalities in family conditions than by unequal school conditions. And because children spend most of their time outside of schools, and because families vary more than schools, families end up being a huge confound for understanding how schools matter. The result is that too often researchers observing differences in outcomes between children attending different schools have misattributed those differences to the schools themselves.

Of course, this view of schools as reflectors of inequality requires a sense of proportion. It's not that schools perfectly mirror society. They can refract the inequalities they receive, sometimes by reducing them, but sometimes they do make them worse. One can find cases where individual schools improve the skills of disadvantaged children to such a degree that achievement gaps are substantially reduced. And one can find cases where the schools children attend are so poor that the experience hinders their educational attainment in a significant way. But it would be a mistake to view those rare cases as indicative of the overall pattern. The reflective part of schools is, by a wide margin, the main story and the statement that schools "reflect more than generate inequality" is true even if we can find evidence that some schools play a role generating inequalities.

For some dimensions of inequality, schools' pernicious role

is more than just a side story—it is the main story. For example, the black/white gap seems to grow faster when school is in versus out, a pattern consistent with the view that schools are exacerbating the problem. But as noted in chapter 3, even in this case, where the evidence against schools is the strongest, we should still put more effort toward reducing large black/white gaps from emerging in the first place. The eighth-grade gaps in math and reading are 78 and 96 percent formed at kindergarten entry, indicating that the bulk of the problem is not school related.

Scholars should continue to explore both compensatory and exacerbatory mechanisms within schools because this kind of work can guide school reforms aimed at reducing inequality. But as currently constituted, schools are not the primary generator of achievement gaps. The possibility that schools play a role reducing inequality is so counterintuitive, however, that it has received very little scholarly attention. I discuss how schools might reduce inequality in the next chapter.

CHAPTER 6

As Helping More than Hurting

In the previous chapter I made the case that we should think
of schools as mostly reflecting rather than generating inequality in broader society. It would be a mistake, however, to conclude that not much of consequence is going on at schools.
Kids learn a great deal while at school, and there are several
school processes that likely shape inequality, both for the good
and the bad. These exacerbatory and compensatory forces
may both be significant, but once the dust clears, it looks like
schools do more to reduce than increase inequality across most
dimensions—a pattern revealed by seasonal comparisons. Overall, therefore, schools should be viewed as helping more than
hurting. Of course, that raises an obvious question—What compensatory processes are we talking about? What could schools
possibly be doing that reduces inequality?

In this chapter I discuss two forms of the compensatory view
of schools, one weak and one strong. The weak form simply
states that school environments are less unequal than nonschool
environments. Schools are compensatory, therefore, just because they're not as unequal as children's homes and neighborhoods. The weak compensatory argument is almost certainly
true, but it is nothing to brag about for schools. In contrast, the

strong form of the compensatory view is that schools actually provide for the needs of disadvantaged children *better* than they do for advantaged children. This is a much higher bar than the weak form of the argument, but it is worth considering because it is consistent with some of the empirical patterns from chapters 1–4. We haven't thought about schools and inequality this way very much, however, and so I offer some theoretical ideas about school mechanisms that might favor disadvantaged children. But first, the weak form.

SCHOOLS AS COMPENSATORY: THE WEAK FORM

One way that schools are compensatory is that they are, simply put, less unequal than home environments—recall figure 3.1. This is important because it means that even unequal schools could be an equalizing force. I call this the "weak" form of the compensatory argument because it doesn't require that schools treat disadvantaged children better than advantaged children, or even equally. It simply notes that, for disadvantaged children, time spent in school might be better than time spent outside of school because nonschool environments are more unequal than school environments. From this perspective, we wouldn't call schools a "great equalizer" but rather a "so-so equalizer."

There is considerable evidence that inequalities outside of school are greater than those in schools. Von Hippel reports this pattern across income inequality, parent/teacher credentials, and class size/family size.[1] Focusing on financial resources is one of the more straightforward ways of comparing variance in school and nonschool environments. Kozol's widely read 1991 book, *Savage Inequalities*, documented drastic disparities in funding between inner city schools and their suburban counterparts.[2] But looking broadly at school funding patterns reveals a different view. The 1971 *Serrano v. Priest* ruling in California prompted a rethinking of the heavy reliance on local taxation and since that time disparities in funding across schools have declined. When adjusted for inflation, expenditures per student from 1995–96 through 2006–07 increased the most in high-poverty districts (35 percent) and increased the least in low-poverty districts (26 percent).[3] On the whole, financial inequality among school districts declined by 20 to 30 percent between 1972 and the 2000s.[4]

The story of family households is the opposite. Financial inequalities among families are substantial and have grown during the last few decades. A child raised in a household of four with income in the lowest 10 percent (of all households) in 2016 lived on $13,234, while one raised in a household of four with income in the highest 10 percent lived on more than ten times that—$161,915. And while income differences are important, differences in wealth also shape children's home environments and are even more extreme. In the U.S., the richest 1 percent hold more wealth than the entire bottom 90 percent. And a 2017 study from the *Institute for Policy Studies* reported that just three Americans (Bill Gates, Warren Buffett, and Jeff Bezos) have as much wealth as the bottom 50 percent of the population.[5] We so often hear about the magnitude of inequality in the U.S. that we can easily lose a sense of proportion. Inequality of wealth in the U.S. is very large (larger than nearly all other countries with advanced economies) and growing. In addition, it is well-established that income and wealth inequality have been increasing during the last few decades.[6]

Schools are more equal than families in other ways too. We sometimes find meaningful differences in the student/teacher ratio where children from advantaged families enjoy smaller classrooms than their counterparts from disadvantaged families. But the child/adult ratio at home likely varies more dramatically when we consider differences in the number of children in the home and, more importantly, the likelihood that a child is raised by a single parent. Consider the following scenario: a disadvantaged child endures a student/teacher ratio of 25:1 while an advantaged child enjoys a 15:1 ratio—a 40 percent smaller child/adult ratio at school. But with three siblings and a single parent, the disadvantaged child's adult/child ratio at home (1:4) is even worse (relatively) than the advantaged child who has one sibling and two parents (1:1). The disadvantaged child's *relative* disadvantage at school, therefore, is smaller, where the child/adult ratio is only 40 percent worse, than at home, where the child/adult ratio is four times as large.[7]

SCHOOLS AS COMPENSATORY: THE STRONG FORM

The weak form of the compensatory argument is attractive, in part because it is so palatable. One can maintain the weak form and largely continue with the view that schools are unequal and need to be reformed. It's a way of acknowledging the seasonal comparison patterns while still maintaining The Assumption.

But the weak form fails to explain some of the empirical patterns from chapters 1–4. For example, if schools were simply less unequal than nonschool environments, we would still expect advantaged children to learn faster than disadvantaged children while in school. After all, they allegedly have two advantages during the nine-month school period—better school and nonschool environments. How is it that, despite both these advantages, they *only* learn at about the same rate as disadvantaged children?

The potential ways in which schools might reduce inequality have been undertheorized. Clearly some school processes that favor children from advantaged backgrounds exist. But to understand how schools matter we need to consider how the *magnitude* of these unfair processes stacks up against the *magnitude* of other school processes that favor children from disadvantaged families. The problem is that virtually no theorists have talked about the ways that schools might be compensatory, and so it's difficult to imagine what these processes might be.

When I discuss schools and inequality in my sociology classes at Ohio State, I first ask the students to think about ways that schools might generate inequality. They are good at this. They respond with enthusiasm and generate a long list of mechanisms (local-based funding, teacher discrimination, teacher quality, curriculum quality, availability of extracurriculars, guidance counselors, etc.) that they can describe in detail. But when I ask them to think about the ways in which schools reduce inequality the room goes silent. What is he talking about?, their confused faces seem to say. Prior to coming to my classroom, the students' ideas about schools and inequality have been so influenced by the dominant narrative that it's difficult for them to even fathom how schools might be compensatory. But the seasonal comparison results suggest that we should think about it.

Below I initiate a discussion of some ways in which schools might be reducing inequality.

Curriculum consolidation. Schools expose children with a wide range of skills to roughly similar material—what I'll call "curriculum consolidation." Social scientists may be more familiar with the term "curriculum differentiation," referring to school practices in which some children are exposed to different material and learning conditions than others, such as ability grouping, tracking, and retention practices. But schools also consolidate children's learning experiences, grouping them together even when their skills are disparate. For example, schools can organize children in many ways, but children's chronological age is the default basis upon which children are typically grouped. This simple policy of organizing children around age is something that we consistently do, but then forget what an important role it likely plays in reducing inequality. To be clear, I do not disagree with this practice but note that the result is a powerful mechanism by which children of widely varying skills are exposed to the same curricular challenges.

Similarly, at a national level, curriculum consolidation occurs to the extent that children across the country are exposed to a similar standardized content. While the U.S. system is less centralized than that of many other countries, there still exist state-level standards that are often comparable and there is a move toward more national standards via the Common Core. The Common Core, now adopted by forty-one states, describes what children should know in reading and mathematics from kindergarten through twelfth grade. This standardization of curriculum can play an important compensatory role by exposing children from a wide range of nonschool environments to similar content. If the Common Core were adopted by all fifty states, schools' compensatory role would be even greater.

Targeting resources toward disadvantaged children. In a similar vein, another way that schools may reduce achievement gaps is by targeting resources toward disadvantaged children. It is important not to overlook the many education policies designed to improve school conditions for disadvantaged children. Title 1, Head Start, the Rehabilitation Act of 1973, and the Americans with Disabilities Act in 1990 all were intended to improve the quality of school experiences for disadvantaged children (and to varying degrees have succeeded in doing so).

And it is worth noting the extent to which investments go into programs aimed at high-performing versus low-performing students. Most school funding comes from local and state sources, so a look at how resources are distributed across children with special needs versus honors students at the state level is informative. As one example, in 2011–12 in Ohio, a school serving a child with a speech impairment received an additional $1,517. The amount rose to $3,849 for developmentally disabled children, and to $16,715 for a child with multiple disabilities. In contrast, schools serving a child identified as gifted received an additional $23.[8] I don't present this as problematic (I like compensatory practices in schools), but I think most people would be surprised to learn of the magnitude in funding differences.

Egalitarian teachers. If you read the social science literature, you would come away with the impression that schools are filled with middle-class teachers determined to keep disadvantaged children from succeeding. Much of the literature draws on Bourdieu's notion of "cultural capital"—the ability to signal affiliation with elites.[9] The idea is that teachers recognize which kids exhibit cultural capital and come from privileged families (by the child's speech, dress, or style or simply by meeting the parents) and they unfairly provide these children with advantages. Perhaps the child is bumped up to a faster reading group when their skills don't quite merit it. Or maybe the child is treated with a softer touch when breaking school rules. And teachers may hold higher expectations of children from privilege, thereby motivating them to learn more. In a widely cited study, DiMaggio found that teachers assigned grades, not just on the basis of the quality of the work, but also by children's knowledge of symphonic music and classic literature.[10] This cultural capital argument has been attractive to academics because it describes an underhanded way in which schools are not really meritocratic. It's not fair if a kid from a rich family gets a detention for fighting while a kid from a poor family gets suspended. And it's not fair if the teacher assigns a rich kid an A in part because the kid listens to Bach.

This notion that American teachers are not meritocratic gatekeepers is a highly attractive view among academicians. But as Paul Kingston, sociologist at the University of Virginia, has pointed out, it's not clear that teachers are as bad as the cultural capital literature suggests.[11] It looks like teachers do reward children who exhibit certain cultural characteristics, but many of these are not arbitrary. For example, teachers prefer students who pay attention and follow directions. Is that unfair? What about DiMaggio's study where it looks like teachers are rewarding kids with arbitrary knowledge of classical music? In that study it's hard to know if privileged children received better grades than disadvantaged children with similar content knowledge because of cultural capital, or because cultural capital is correlated with some other unmeasured advantage in the home environment. The same weakness we uncovered in the traditional studies of schools—correlation does not equal causation—applies here. Kingston walks through a wide range of cultural capital studies and concludes that the claims represent an "unfulfilled promise." That's not to say that there is no evidence that teachers treat children unfairly, but rather that when analyzed closely it is more modest than many realize.

The discriminatory behavior that teachers do exhibit, and they surely are imperfect in this way, may also be countered by significant egalitarian behavior. While much is made of teacher behavior that exacerbates inequality, it is worth considering that these instances may be countered by a bigger pattern— teachers' general egalitarian approach. The kinds of people attracted to teaching are distinct from the general population— they are more interested in helping others and more likely to endorse relatively egalitarian views than most. For example, in the General Social Survey data, 47 percent of nonteachers said that "lack of effort" is a "very important" reason why some people are poor, compared to just 32 percent of teachers. And a national survey of teachers found that when asked who was most likely to receive one-on-one attention, 80 percent of teachers said "academically struggling students" while just 5 percent said "academically advanced" students.[12] It may be that teachers sometimes favor children from advantaged families under some conditions, but most research studies fail to provide a broad enough scope to assess the possibility that, overall, teacher behaviors exacerbating inequality are outweighed by a greater tendency to favor the disadvantaged. It's difficult to know if this is how the world works because few studies have considered it, but as we build theory to explain how schools might be compensatory, I think this is one plausible mechanism.

Does schools' compensatory power extend beyond cognitive skills? One frequently raised argument for why the seasonal comparison research does not undermine The Assumption is that schools reproduce inequality in many other ways, beyond math and reading skills. Schools serving advantaged children, for example, tend to train students in ways that prepare them for high-income jobs. They emphasize learning how to synthesize information, think critically, and engage in reasoned debate. In contrast, schools serving disadvantaged children tend to focus on rote memory skills, following strict rules, and the kinds of skills useful in lower-level jobs. Many researchers have documented these kinds of differences in schools serving advantaged versus disadvantaged children.[13]

It is difficult to assess exactly how schools matter for all skills relevant to the job world, but we have studied how exposure to school shapes gaps in social and behavioral skills or "citizenship" in the classroom (e.g., paying attention, completing work on time, getting along with peers). It is well known that children arrive at kindergarten with large gaps in these skills. High-SES, female, and white children have much higher social and behavioral skills than low-SES, male, and black children. One argument is that schools make the gaps between these groups even worse, because advantaged children enjoy better teachers and peers. But it is also possible that differences in social and behavioral skills are largely developed outside of the school, in the home environment, and that schools then largely reflect the home environments of students they serve. As I noted earlier, my colleagues and I assessed how teachers' ratings of children's social and behavioral skills changed while in school versus out.

Teachers evaluated children in terms of a set of learning behaviors (e.g., keeps belongings organized; shows eagerness to learn new things; works independently; easily adapts to changes in routine; persists in completing tasks; pays attention well; and follows classroom rules). We found that gaps in these social and behavioral skills were large across SES, race, and gender at kindergarten entry, but there was little evidence that the gaps increased faster when school was in versus out of session between kindergarten and second grade. This is one of the only studies applying a seasonal comparison method to outcomes like social and behavioral skills, but it is telling that it provides no support for the position that schools are pernicious in ways beyond cognitive skills.[14]

Scholars have also considered how exposure to schools affects obesity patterns using seasonal methods. One argument is that schools have become "obesity zones" because of their poor-quality lunches and lack of consistent recess and physical education. But the seasonal studies suggest that children gain BMI (body mass index) faster when school is out than when in and that gaps in BMI across socioeconomic status and race tend to grow fastest in the summers.[15] Schools, with all their warts, do more to reduce than increase obesity and gaps in BMI between advantaged and disadvantaged children. That is not to say that school lunches are great, but rather that the typical kid's health (in terms of BMI gain) is better when attending school than not.

The fact that schools look either compensatory or neutral with respect to socioeconomic status whenever we analyze outcomes with seasonal comparison methods raises the possibility that schools operate in a different manner than the dominant narrative assumes. It's worth noting that, prior to using seasonal comparison methods, most scholars believed that schools increase SES-based achievement gaps. The results of seasonal comparison studies forced them to rethink this view. Before we assume that schools necessarily create inequalities in other ways, we should think about whether we're making the same mistake scholars made before—overestimating the role schools play in shaping inequality.

CONCLUSION

After the Coleman Report noted that schools play only a small role in explaining achievement gaps, some commentators mistakenly concluded that Coleman had claimed that schools don't matter. That conclusion was wrong in the 1960s and it's still wrong. Children learn faster in school than out, a fact that should be comforting to both parents and taxpayers in general. But two things can be true at the same time: (1) schools can promote learning very effectively, and (2) schools can play very little role generating inequality. The reason they can both be true is because of the big surprise from chapter 3—schools serving advantaged children promote about the same amount of school-based learning as schools serving disadvantaged children.

When we analyze schools' overall effect on skill inequality, they appear to do more to help than hurt. This conclusion is not diminished by the fact that some school characteristics may make inequality worse. An accurate understanding of schools requires that we weigh the forces that make inequality worse (exacerbatory) against those that reduce it (compensatory). Seasonal comparison studies are well suited for this task while most other research designs simply focus on exacerbatory mechanisms. The reason seasonal studies are so powerful, therefore, is that they don't make the mistake of overlooking the possibility that schools are in some ways compensatory.

So if the news about schools is better than we thought, why do we continue to blame them? This has puzzled me for a while. I offer my thoughts in the next chapter.

CHAPTER 7
A *Frida Sofia* Problem

After a disastrous 7.1-magnitude earthquake on September 19, 2017, Mexico became engrossed in the rescue of Frida Sofia, a twelve-year-old girl attending Enrique Rebsamen School near Mexico City. The school had collapsed and many students and teachers were killed. Rescue workers heard her weak voice but officials reported that they were having difficulty pinpointing her location. The girl had told rescue workers that her name was Frida Sofia. The entire country held its breath, following every news report and social media post.

There was just one problem. It turned out that there wasn't any Frida Sofia. There were no records of a girl with that name attending the school. After these facts emerged, officials started backtracking their statements, which had relied on those of rescue workers. Why had several rescue workers given details of a young girl named Frida Sofia caught in the rubble? Some of the mistakes are easily understood. The thermal cameras used to find survivors can produce false positives. Maybe that happened. And the fingers that rescuers reported seeing might have been those of a fifty-eight-year-old woman whose body was found in the rubble.

But why did rescue workers report talking to a girl, and why did they report that she told them her name was Frida Sofia? These details weren't true, and yet they were given to a reporter and then widely circulated. Instead of verifying the information, the reporters and the Mexican officials relayed it to the public, perpetuating the mistake for days.[1]

One answer for why this fictitious girl's story developed and received so much attention is that everyone wanted it to be true. The earthquake had killed 370 people and injured 6,000 more. The country was desperate for good news and the potential survival of this young girl gave everyone hope. As social scientists have demonstrated repeatedly, when we really want something to be true, we're not nearly as good at determining whether it really is.

So what does the Frida Sofia problem have to do with schools and inequality? Am I suggesting that people really want a school-based explanation for inequality? Yes, that's exactly what I'm saying. To clarify, it's not that people *want* schools to increase inequality, but rather they want a school-based explanation for inequality. And unfortunately for schools, both liberal and conservative political groups are motivated in this way (for different reasons of course). When people want a certain explanation to be true, they are prone to downplaying contrary evidence.

The problem may be just as prevalent among academicians as it is among the general public. In the past decade I've presented the patterns in chapters 1–4 to more than a dozen audiences at universities and research institutes and the responses often follow predictable stages of resistance. At stage one there is surprise about the evidence. Audience members are shocked to learn that 87 percent of eighteen-year-old's time awake is spent outside of school and they didn't realize that achievement gaps form mostly during early childhood. They didn't know that socioeconomic gaps in math and reading are rather stable when children are in school (and sometimes even grow faster when school is out than in) and they are stunned by the impact results indicating that there is about the same amount of school-based learning in schools serving advantaged versus disadvantaged children. They look for ways in which these patterns could all be wrong, the denial stage, but the fact that inequality is mostly formed prior to formal schooling is too difficult to explain.

At stage two the conversation shifts toward a critique of cognitive skills. Skeptics acknowledge the patterns for reading and math skills but argue that schools probably increase inequality in lots of other ways. Of course, this may be true and it's difficult to know based on current evidence because so much of it fails to isolate school effects persuasively. So, while it may be possible that schools promote inequality in many ways other than cognitive skills, it is important to have some humility regarding how confidently we maintain that position. As noted earlier, when we do extend the seasonal comparison method (or other more rigorous methods) to other outcomes, like social and behavioral skills and body mass index, we end up with a more favorable view of schools. If we applied the seasonal comparison method to an even broader array of dependent variables, we might be less confident that schools promote inequality in ways other than cognitive skills.

Stage three resistance is about how to address inequality. Some scholars will acknowledge everything about stages one and two, but still insist that school reform is the way to go. It's the primary lever that we have, they point out, and so we should do what we can with it. And in this stage, they acknowledge that schools do not influence inequality much, but they insist that schools serving disadvantaged children could be better. Of course, they are right, that schools serving disadvantaged children could be better. The real question is whether school reform is the optimal approach for reducing achievement gaps.

I conclude that we really need to reform the distribution of rewards in the broader society. They respond that we can't do that—we can't change families, so we should just stick with something possible, like school reform. I posit that if we restrict ourselves to only studying school reform (because we view that as the only lever we can manipulate) and avoid studying what really produces achievement gaps (inequality in the broader society) because we worry that it is impossible to change politically, then we contribute to the likelihood that it won't change. My view is that social scientists should focus on explaining how the world actually operates rather than avoid talking about what really produces inequality because we think it can't be changed.

This resistance sequence has made me wonder why The Assumption is so difficult to challenge. Why are schools such an attractive villain? I don't think that the people questioning the evidence are bad people, but they are reluctant to let go of the dominant narrative about schools. It would be one thing if the reason was because they had issues with whether the ECLS-K item-response theory scales of reading can be considered truly interval, or if they questioned whether nonschool investments in children are constant across seasons, or if they thought that the approach scholars use to model the overlap days between test dates and the beginnings and ends of school years was insufficient. Seasonal comparison research is not perfect and may produce errant estimates for all of these reasons (see appendix B for more discussion on the seasonal comparison method). But while many have resisted the empirical patterns in chapters 1–4 and remain committed to The Assumption, the quality of evidence doesn't seem to be the obstacle. They resist for more complicated reasons.

I believe that this opposition stems from several factors. First, scholars critical of schools tend to frame the question differently from seasonal comparison scholars. Below I'll explain why framing matters so much. Second, the American value of small government serves us well in some ways, but when pushed too far it begins to warp our understanding of what causes what. I believe that our understanding of how schools influence inequality has been distorted, in part, because of our value against state action. Third, the backlash to the 1965 Moynihan Report led social scientists to become especially sensitive to accusations of "blaming the victim." This was a good thing in part, but not in full because researchers began shying away from research that might direct attention to challenges in disadvantaged families. The result has been a slanted view that fails to recognize a reality—early childhood family conditions are critical to shaping children's development and achievement gaps. Finally, the fact that teachers are mostly women makes schools especially vulnerable to criticism, something male-dominated occupations (like police officers) don't endure to the same degree.

SCHOOLS AND INEQUALITY: STUCK WITHIN THE TRADITIONAL FRAMING

Perhaps the main reason The Assumption persists is that the way the question is usually framed doesn't give schools a chance. The typical scholar asks, "Are there aspects of schools that promote inequality?" The answer is almost certainly yes. After numerous scholars asking the question this way identify a wide array of school characteristics that widen inequality, the entire field believes the dominant narrative.

To understand why the answer here is largely determined by the framing, consider an analogy. Imagine a group of baseball fans who watch recordings of the games where all the footage of their team at bat has been deleted so that they only observe the times when their team is in the field playing defense. In addition, they never know whether their team wins these games, just how they did when in the field with the other team at bat.

Now imagine discussing the team with these fans over a beer. They might have a few good things to say, perhaps they've seen some good pitching and some great defensive plays, but they are more likely to be frustrated fans than if they watched the entire games. They never get to enjoy watching one of their players steal a base, or stretch a double into a triple, or hit a homerun. They never see their team score a run. And, if you asked them how the team is doing it would be no surprise if they expressed an overly pessimistic view. Just look at all the runs the team is giving up!

These odd fans are not so different from the scholars who study schools and inequality. Asking "Are there aspects of schools that increase inequality?" is like watching a baseball team in the field and asking, "Do they ever mess up?" The way the question is framed guarantees an affirmative answer. Now to be fair, education scholars haven't focused exclusively on the negative, but they have certainly targeted it. It's not hard to find imperfections in schools, especially when you look hard, and so education scholarship presents this mostly one-sided view. When framed this way, schools don't have a chance.

As a result of this framing, the weaknesses of our schools serving disadvantaged children come to dominant the public's mind. For example, a widely read 2007 *New York Times* article described how New York City houses its problem teachers in a "rubber room" where there are no windows and no internet connection, and where they must stay each day until their disciplinary procedures are complete.[2] Some of them stay there for years. In 2010 the city spent over $30 million in salary to more than five hundred teachers who spent their days in the rubber room.[3] These poor-performing teachers are difficult to fire because they are protected by the powerful teachers' union.

This is the side of education that we often hear about in the news. We learn about the teacher who falls asleep in class or is frequently late or absent. We hear about the high school with 25 percent graduation rates. But these horror stories, as bad as they are, do not represent the main story. Bad schools and bad teachers make good headlines. We rarely see headlines like "Another day of solid reading gains at Sunnybrook Elementary School," and yet that more accurately describes what typically goes on.

Our overly critical view of schools is revealed by the Phi Delta Kappan polls each year. Most parents, around 70 percent, assign a letter grade of A or B to their child's school but rate the nation's schools with a C or D. Why do people view the overall education system so poorly, even though they are generally happy with their own school? They know that their own child enjoys school, but they seem to be influenced by The Assumption and so, even though their own experience is positive, they end up believing that the nation's schools are problematic.

This traditional framing has limited value for understanding how schools influence inequality. Just like you can't really know if a baseball team is doing well if you only watch them play defense, you can't really tell what schools' overall contribution to inequality is if you only focus on those aspects of schools that increase inequality. Because this framing lacks a way of comparing the magnitude of school mechanisms that make inequality worse with those that reduce it, it almost guarantees that researchers will conclude that schools make inequality worse. And because most people believe this about schools in the first place, few people think about how the framing limits the possible answer.

An alternative framing is "How does exposure to schooling affect inequality?" Note that this second framing focuses on how the institution of schooling *overall* matters. Going back to the baseball analogy, instead of just watching the team play defense we would instead ask "Who had more runs at the end of the game?" And instead of asking whether there are mechanisms within schools that promote inequality (surely there are) we would ask, When exposed to schools, how does inequality change?

This exposure approach to understanding how schools matter automatically takes a bigger-picture view. It does not deny that some school mechanisms might contribute to inequality, but it also does not deny that some might reduce inequality. The advantage to this framing is that it is better positioned to provide a sense of proportion. If there exist within schools both mechanisms that exacerbate inequality and those that compensate for inequality, this approach weighs them against each other and reveals which is stronger. But if schools' overall effect is neutral or even compensatory, this framing can reveal that too. In contrast, the first framing does not provide schools much of a chance because it lacks proportion — scholars can almost always find some school mechanisms that exacerbate inequality.

OUR VALUE FOR LIMITED GOVERNMENT

While the framing issue is important, another reason Americans cling to The Assumption is because it allows them to maintain their value for limited government. This is a case where some people may not care to hear about the real source of achievement gaps because the answer probably requires state intervention in a way that they don't want. David Ropiek pointed out in his 2010 *Atlantic* article "Global Warming: No Big Deal?"[4] that some groups of people, those comfortable with hierarchy and the status quo and uncomfortable with significant state intervention, are more likely to be skeptical of climate change. The reason, he argued, had little to do with the actual facts and more about the kinds of solutions required for the problem. If climate change is real, it would require some kind of government approach to addressing the problem, and if you don't want the government to be bigger, then you don't want climate change to be real. Similarly, if you want the smallest government possible, The Assumption is attractive because it focuses government energy on the schools, where it can be restricted, rather than directed toward reducing inequality in broader society, which would likely require a larger welfare state.[5]

After the Great Depression, the U.S. faced a serious problem. Capitalism wasn't working. It produced too much inequality and led to booms and busts, and the loss of so many jobs led to a great deal of human misery. Roosevelt's New Deal initiated a different relationship between government and the market, one where government regulated the market more and provided for the well-being of vulnerable citizens. The way that the government did this was, at first, considered quite broad. The government initiated Social Security, and later, Medicare and programs designed to keep children from going hungry. But while most modern societies experienced this same growth in the state during the 1930s and 1940s, the U.S. departed from other countries in a significant way. Other countries saw education policy as just part of a broader role for government, while in the U.S. the view increasingly shifted toward elevating school-based solutions over other ones, in what Havey Kantor and Robert Lowe call "educationalizing the welfare state."[6]

Why did the U.S. emphasize education so much more than other countries? Tracy Steffes provides a compelling answer. In *School, Society, and State*, she notes that

part of the answer to the question of why Americans invested in education may be found in how it resonated with American political culture and values, including long-cherished myths about progress, individualism, merit, and opportunity. It was an individualistic project of self-improvement, an avenue for individual and collective progress. Schooling was not a form of charity or relief; it was an enabling institution that purported to maintain fairness and opportunity so that any individual could rise through his or her own effort and talent. In a nation where most people were invested in the American Dream of mobility, the popular demand was for government to safeguard this promise rather than compensate for its failures.[7]

Partly because of this value for a weak central government, Americans are especially prone to look for school-based solutions to social problems. They can stomach investments in schools more than programs that might look like handouts because at least schools require students to work hard. As a result, people in the U.S. are more reluctant than Canadians or Europeans to help disadvantaged families via nonschool policies (e.g., increasing the minimum wage, greater public transportation, parental leave, broader access to health care, proworker legislation, and reducing mass incarceration).[8] U.S. antistatism has helped produce a smaller, more school-centric, welfare system.

On its surface, this may not sound too bad. Holding people accountable for their actions, for example, seems like a great idea. But the value for small government ends up serving us poorly when it misdirects our attention away from the real sources of the problem. When it comes to achievement gaps, for example, it prompts us to value school-based solutions too much and overlook the ways that other government decisions have shaped inequality outside of schools.

FEAR OF "BLAMING THE VICTIM"

If Americans are so caught up on individualism, then why not focus their attention on the family, which is a smaller and more personal institution than schools? To understand why scholars have been reluctant to describe families as contributing to inequalities we need to revisit another report from the 1960s: *The Moynihan Report.*

In the 1960s, the War on Poverty faced some serious obstacles. Many people believed that poverty was simply a product of lazy people and the way to fix it was to fix those people. Get them off their butts and working more and poverty would go away, was the idea. Fortunately, a more contextual perspective started to gain prominence and policymakers began to identify how structural problems, like the lack of economic opportunity and racism, stressed families and were root sources of the problem. This more sophisticated understanding recognized that you probably wouldn't get very far by just telling poor people to behave better; you were going to need to address these larger issues.

This was the contextual story that came out of a report produced in 1965 by Daniel Patrick Moynihan, a young assistant secretary of labor. The Moynihan Report (its official title was *The Negro Family: The Case for National Action*) located the problems of the black family in the economy. Moynihan made the case for a national jobs program that would provide education, training, and apprenticeship programs and full employment for all able-bodied workers. Moynihan thought that this was the kind of solution that would promote stability in the black family.

You would think that this message would have been embraced by progressives but the report's main message was overwhelmed by a few provocative and offensive sentences. Moynihan talked about a "tangle of pathology" in the black family that led to the persistence of black poverty across generations. And the author described female-headed households as "pathological." Moynihan even posited that the matriarchal character of the black family prevents black males from fulfilling "the very essence of the male animal from the bantam rooster to the four star general . . . to strut."[9]

The headlines were about Moynihan calling the black family pathological and blaming it for the emergence of ghettos while the big-picture structural argument was lost. The press coverage suggested that Moynihan was bashing the black family and blaming educational failure, joblessness, and criminality on black matriarchy. William Ryan, writing in *The Nation*, coined the term "blaming the victim" to describe Moynihan's approach.[10] The criticism mounted from the left; the black power movement resented the image of humiliated black men and the emerging feminists resented the notion of pairing matriarchy and pathology.

Social scientists learned a lesson from all of this—be very careful when talking about the disadvantaged. This was, of course, a good lesson to learn but the problem was that they shifted away from studying the realities of family life and how much it mattered. The Moynihan Report became the poster child example of blaming the victim. Rather than acknowledging that some family conditions are better for children than others, social scientists failed to acknowledge fully the challenges of single parenthood or the difficulties of urban poverty. Better to just not talk about it than get criticized like Moynihan. Instead, scholars portrayed the disadvantaged as heroic in their efforts to cope with the extreme circumstances they faced. They avoided the challenging parts of poor, segregated urban life and focused more on the resilience of the poor, which was real, but left untold the main story.

This intellectual atmosphere ended up producing a generation of social scientists who were gun shy about discussing the family's real role in reproducing inequality. The notion that inequality might be reproduced, at least in part, by the conditions that children experience within the family was just too sensitive to discuss. Social scientists struggled to acknowledge that some features of disadvantaged families were not that great for children. Sociologists Douglas Massey and Robert Sampson noted, "The possibility that family disruption, multi-partner childbearing, and tenuous attachment by fathers might have negative effects on children became taboo. In the end, the hypothesis that single parenthood might interact with structural features of American society to exacerbate the detrimental effects of joblessness, discrimination, and segregation was set aside."[11]

That is not to say that family sociology disappeared altogether but rather that it became a smaller part of the story about how inequality is reproduced. The pendulum swung far away from the family. Whereas the old narrative, one emphasized by Moynihan, described how structural inequalities, like residential segregation and job discrimination shaped family conditions which then shaped children's development and reproduced inequality, the newer story diminished the role of family conditions altogether. As the sociologist Douglas Massey explained years later, Moynihan's sin was that he "implied that under certain circumstances, the behavior of poor people might contribute to the perpetuation of their poverty, and for this heresy . . . [he was] excoriated by liberals throughout the social science establishment. The calumny . . . had a chilling effect on social science over the next two decades. Sociologists avoided studying controversial issues related to race, culture, and intelligence, and those who insisted on investigating such unpopular notions generally encountered resistance and ostracism."[12]

If social scientists couldn't talk about how disadvantage was perpetuated through family conditions, then someone had to explain how poverty persisted. Rather than linking family conditions to broader structural challenges, like Moynihan did, some scholars attributed them to an overly generous welfare system, poor cultural values, or, worst of all, genetic inferiority.[13] These scholars saw the black family as the problem itself while Moynihan had seen problems within the black family as the end result of larger structural issues. The irony in all of this is thick. Moynihan's report was meant to encourage policies that would change the structural conditions in society and improve the stability of black families, but several insensitive phrasings in the report produced a response that was so hostile that it ended up generating a *less* structural view of poverty.

Social scientists lacked nuance in their response to the Moynihan Report. Their condemnation of the report threw out the good with the bad and set social science on a suboptimal path for several decades—a path that undervalued what goes on within families. In short, a sense of proportion was lost. Scholars could talk about structure but they couldn't acknowledge what was going on within families that contributed to the perpetuation of inequality, even if they recognized that family conditions were shaped by structure. Of course, this new story from social scientists didn't feel right to many people because it wasn't, and social scientists' accounts of inequality had less and less influence on public debate. Without the family to blame, social scientists looked elsewhere to understand how inequality persists. Schools were a safer target.

GENDER AND THE VULNERABILITY OF SCHOOLS

There is another reason I think schools take so much grief—they are dominated by women. If women enjoyed the same resources and status as men this wouldn't be such a problem, but they don't. Seventy-seven percent of American public school teachers were female in 2015–16 and the percentage of female teachers increases to nearly 90 percent at the elementary level.[14] The fact that most teachers are women may be a reason why schools receive so much criticism, and also why teachers' attempts to unionize and protect their interests are so often maligned. Consider the way male-dominated occupations are viewed. When fires break out we don't necessarily develop accountability systems to evaluate firefighters. And not only are teachers paid poorly, but they are held responsible for outcomes in a way that we don't apply to other, male-dominated occupations. Scholars have pointed out that occupations that become more feminized tend to decline in pay.[15] The more women enter a field, the more status that field loses. The devaluation of women and the maintenance of The Assumption are not unrelated.

CONCLUSION

In this chapter I considered a puzzle—if the evidence against The Assumption is so damning, why does it persist? I offered four reasons: (1) framing, (2) our value for limited government, (3) the backlash to the Moynihan Report, and (4) the vulnerability of a female-dominated occupation (teachers). This perfect storm of conditions has made American schools uniquely vulnerable to criticism and created the cultural atmosphere that can maintain The Assumption despite contrary evidence.[16]

We may also blame schools because the dominant narrative is one of the few issues on which liberals and conservatives agree. They both think that unequal schools are an engine of inequality. That is remarkable, given how polarized political discourse is in so many other areas. Of course, liberals and conservatives have different solutions to the problem—liberals want to equalize resources while conservatives tout market principles—but most importantly they both identify schools as increasing inequality. That kind of political consensus has resulted in the dominant narrative surviving with little scrutiny.

Finally, I think The Assumption persists in part because the seasonal comparison story is dry and fails to excite the passions. When my undergraduate students are exposed to the unfairness of resource distribution across schools they are inspired. Some of them want to join Teach for America or fight for new legislation. And they love reading Kozol's *Savage Inequalities*, which artfully describes differences in schools serving advantaged and disadvantaged children. But make them read Entwisle and Alexander's "Summer Setback" article, which more accurately describes the big picture story, and they yawn. The problem is that no one gets inspired when they hear the seasonal comparison story. No one stands up and says "amen" when they learn that SES-based gaps in math and reading are completely formed before formal schooling begins. Trying to persuade people that schools don't cause as much inequality as we thought is like trying to market a movie based on a villain who turns out to be an ok guy. It's much more interesting if Voldemort is just evil. Maintaining The Assumption allows us to keep our villain. But it's the wrong villain and this mistake comes with costs, the subject of the next chapter.

CHAPTER 8
The Costly Assumption

We should reconsider the view that schools are an engine of inequality because it is not serving us well. The patterns I discussed in chapters 1–4 are difficult to explain from that position and merit further discussion. It's not easy to evaluate deeply held views, but it is costly to simply press on with the dominant narrative. Of course, one could read this book and conclude that The Assumption is not really that big a problem. Maybe we're blaming schools too much for inequality, the argument would go, but we still need to blame them some and so, at its worst, we end up targeting school inequalities a little more than we should. Is that such a bad thing?

I acknowledge that The Assumption is only mostly wrong, not completely wrong. Meaningful inequalities in American schools exist that run counter to our value of equal opportunity. To their credit, researchers shaped by the dominant narrative have identified unfair teacher practices, disparities in classroom size, and ability grouping and tracking processes that all may increase inequality. And although schools may not do much to increase SES-based achievement gaps, they may be promoting racial ones. For these reasons, we should continue to make special efforts to improve the schools serving disadvantaged children.

My thesis should be understood as proportionate—not that combatting inequality via schools is completely misguided, but rather that we currently put too much emphasis on schools and too little on early childhood. Perhaps The Assumption's greatest cost is the way it promotes an overly critical view of schools and thereby diverts attention away from the root sources of inequality. In that way the direct costs of combatting inequality via school reform may be modest, but the indirect costs much greater. A school-centric approach to reducing achievement gaps can result in spending resources in a suboptimal way. Here are a couple examples of people with resources wanting to reduce inequality via schools, but learning the hard way that the traditional story about schools is wrong.

RICH GUYS TRYING TO REDUCE ACHIEVEMENT GAPS

You would think that with their combination of money and business success, Bill Gates and Mark Zuckerberg could figure out how to reduce achievement gaps. But while they have both been highly successful in business, they have had little success trying to reduce inequality via schools. This isn't so much because money doesn't matter at all or that business principles can never succeed in schools, but rather because they misdiagnosed the problem. They assumed that the problem begins with the schools when it really is about economic and racial stratification outside of schools.

Let's start with the Bill and Melinda Gates Foundation. They've been involved in improving schools for several years. At first, they believed that small schools were the key. They funded the reorganization of many large high schools into smaller ones, the idea being that these smaller environments could address students' specific needs more directly. The reasoning was that if you make the poorest schools look like their high-performing counterparts, you could produce similar outcomes. The idea wasn't bad but it turned out that it was very expensive and less effective than anticipated.[1] After considerable money and resources were spent splitting large schools into small ones, the Gates people abandoned the strategy.[2]

They then pivoted and focused on teacher quality. Perhaps if they could identify good teachers and get more of them to teach at schools serving disadvantaged children, they could reduce inequality. They pursued this for a while but then realized that this strategy wasn't going to work either. The problem is that good teachers weren't just concentrated in schools serving advantaged kids. As I've mentioned before, teacher quality is much more evenly distributed than most people realize and so it hardly explains any inequality. Eventually the Gates Foundation moved on to other issues unrelated to education, like improving sanitation systems and providing vaccinations in developing countries. Schools were just too hard.

There must be something about having a few extra billion dollars sitting around that makes people want to reform schools because, a few years later, Facebook's CEO Mark Zuckerberg went down the same path. In 2008 the Newark, New Jersey, city school system got great news. Zuckerberg had decided to donate a $100 million to the district, which would be matched by gifts from individuals and foundations, resulting in $200 million for the Newark Public School District. It was such a big deal that they announced it on *The Oprah Winfrey Show*. The Newark schools were some of the poorest-performing in the country. Fewer than 40 percent of the students in third through eighth grades were reading or doing math at grade level, and nearly half of the system's students dropped out before high school graduation. What Zuckerberg and then-mayor Corey Booker wanted to do was not just improve Newark's schools, but provide a model for how to create excellent urban school districts for the country within five years. It was a noble goal.[3]

Did the Newark public schools become that model for all of America? No. After a few years the money was gone and there was little to show for it. The students improved somewhat in English but declined in math. Most of the money had gone to highly paid consultants and to fulfilling an existing teachers' contract. Some would blame the teachers' unions for resisting the kind of reform necessary to reward the best teachers and improve the schools. Others would blame the controversial superintendent, Cami Anderson, who failed to develop the public consensus needed for implementing reforms. In the end, the money was gone and there was no model urban school district to show the rest of the country.

To their credit, these rich guys seem to learn from their mistakes. Zuckerberg and his wife, Priscilla Chan, later donated $120 million to high-poverty schools in the San Francisco Bay area, but this time with the goal of helping more than just the schools. As *New York Times* writer Alex Kotlowitz notes, "Zuckerberg came to recognize that school reform alone isn't enough, that if we're going to make a difference in the classroom, we also need to make a difference in the lives of these children, many of whom struggle against the debilitating effects of poverty and trauma."[4] It took $100 million to learn the lesson, but Zuckerberg moved toward viewing schools as more reflectors than generators of inequality.

THE NEVER-ENDING QUEST TO REFORM SCHOOLS

The Assumption not only shaped Gates's and Zuckerberg's efforts, it also shapes the story of many urban school districts around the country that are in a continuous state of reform. That schools mostly reflect society's larger inequalities is part of why it has been so difficult to resolve social problems like achievement gaps via school reform. But because the dominant narrative is so strong, school reform is the approach most widely endorsed and so we see the same school reform efforts over and over again in urban school districts around the country. And unfortunately, these efforts typically fail.

When I moved to Columbus, Ohio, in 1994 it was obvious that the Columbus City School District was struggling. Its reputation was poor with graduation rates and test scores among the lowest in the state. But in the last quarter century there has been considerable energy invested in improving the school district. New superintendents arrived with catchy slogans. In 1995 it was Larry Mixon, who brought "Total Quality Management" principles to the job. Two years later it was Rosa Smith, who touted a three-pronged strategy aimed at increasing academic achievement, operating more efficiently, and raising hope and trust. In 2001 came Gene Harris, who encouraged staff to "Step Up" and "Make Academic Achievement Happen."

Unfortunately, these efforts have not done much. Sure, we can find some good news if we cherry-pick a few choice outcomes. But if we take a broader look we mostly see the same disappointing results, which is why the district received an F report card from the state of Ohio in 2018. In many ways, the Columbus City School District is in the same place it was twenty-five years ago.

It would be one thing if the discouraging news from Columbus was unique, but unfortunately it is not. The dominant story across the country, by far, is that urban school districts continue to struggle in spite of school reforms. Every few years a new superintendent comes in with a hopeful message and new ideas, but not much changes. A common explanation for the problem is that these districts are run inefficiently. If the administrators were more professional and the teachers more dedicated, the argument goes, these poorly performing schools would produce better outcomes. And there's always just enough truth to that, even if it's just a little, to allow that view to persist.

But the big reason these school districts continue to struggle, year after year, is much more about the disadvantaged students they serve than it is about what they do with them. That is not to say that the urban districts are perfect. Far from it. In 2012, Columbus, like several other urban school districts, had its own data-rigging scandal, cooking the numbers to make the district look better. But the dominant reason the urban districts continue to perform poorly on report cards is because the tools used to evaluate them gauge not just how well the school is doing, but also the stressed homes and neighborhoods the children experience. As long as the children these schools serve continue to endure difficult nonschool environments, demonstrating consistent and sustainable academic gains is very difficult. As a result, schools serving disadvantaged children consistently rate as the poorest schools.

Ohio's assessment tool just makes the problem worse. The report card for schools is constructed from six indicators and not a single one of them gauges performance independent of children's nonschool environments. First is *achievement*, which is based on the percentage of students who pass state tests. Of course, how well students do on achievement tests (at one point in time) is a mix of both school and nonschool factors. Recall figure 2.1 and how achievement gaps are almost entirely in place at kindergarten entry. By far, the biggest determinant of whether a school produces high or low test scores is the income level of the students' families it serves. Second is the extent to which a district *closes achievement gaps* among subgroups. But performance on this indicator can also be influenced by factors out of the schools' control. For example, school A might struggle to close gaps between advantaged and disadvantaged children largely because a local plant closed down, raising unemployment and stressing many low-income families. School B might produce gap closings because the plant moved to its district, raising employment opportunities and lowering stress among low-income families. Third, schools are gauged by the degree to which the school *improved at-risk K-3 readers*. This measures how well a school raises the reading proficiency rate of a subset of its K-3 readers. Of course, it is much easier to make progress on this indicator if serving children who go home each evening to parents who reinforce the school goals. Fourth, schools are evaluated on their *progress*, an indicator based on how much growth students exhibit on math and reading tests. This kind of indicator is better than most at isolating how schools matter, but again, growth is easier in schools where students enjoy home environments that also promote learning (e.g., good health care, stable homes, parents that reinforce academic concepts). Fifth, the *graduation rate* constitutes a component of the district's grade. But this is only a measure of school quality if the likelihood of a child's on-time graduation has nothing to do with the stress they experience at home, the access they have to health care, or the quality of their neighborhood. Finally, districts are evaluated on whether their students are *prepared for success*. This indicator gauges the percentage of students at a school viewed as ready to succeed after high school—either in work or at college—and is determined by how well the students performed on the ACT or SAT and whether they earned a 3 or higher on at least one AP exam. Again, the strong link between poverty and scores on standardized tests makes it clear that this outcome is only partly within the control of the school.[5]

These report cards "are designed to give parents, communities, educators, and policymakers information about the performance of districts and school," but what they really do is mix important factors outside of school with what is going on inside the schools in unknown ways. Part of the reason why Columbus city schools received an overall grade of F in 2018 from the state of Ohio was that only 3 percent earned a score of 3 or better on an AP exam. Recall that children spend 87 percent of their waking hours outside of school. Any report card that ignores that

87 percent, or acknowledges it only in part, provides a distorted view of how well the schools are actually doing. Ohio's report cards are likely a better mirror of the poor conditions that exist in Columbus's neighborhoods than an accurate measurement of the quality of what occurs within their schools.

What would make for a better school report card? Any good report card would benefit from following philosopher John Rawls's advice for creating the principles for a fair society. Rawls asked us to imagine what a fair world would look like. He suggested that citizens being asked to create the rules for this society should make them from a "veil of ignorance," meaning that they would not know what gender, race, abilities, tastes, or wealth they would be born into. Rawls argued that a fair society would be the kind that we would construct and then be ok with the possibility of being randomly assigned to any position within that society.[6]

Similarly, a fair system for evaluating schools needs to be one where principals and teachers would be willing to be randomly assigned to any school and feel confident that they would then be evaluated accurately for their performance. Does anyone think that we have that now? Definitely not. Teachers and principals know we don't; it's part of why they prefer teaching children from advantaged backgrounds. They know it's easier. Our current evaluation tools say more about the children a school serves than the quality of what occurs within the classroom. In practice I believe that a better report card might draw on a seasonal design and gauge schools' impact (as discussed in chapter 4), but even impact scores should be just one component of effective evaluation.[7]

THE GREAT DISTRACTOR

Perhaps the biggest cost of The Assumption is how it diverts our attention away from the root source of inequality—the uneven distribution of rewards in broader society. We don't have the kind of society John Rawls saw as fair—one where we'd happy to be randomly assigned any gender, race, set of skills, or amount of wealth. We know that all of those characteristics currently shape success in unfair ways and that, as American society is currently constructed, we don't always get what we deserve. That can change. We can make a fairer society. But to do so we'll have to direct our energies toward the real sources of inequality, not schools.

But maybe schools could be used to fix inequality even if they didn't create it. Maybe they really do mostly reflect rather than generate inequality, but they could be the best lever for reducing inequality anyway. Some studies show that sending disadvantaged children to high-flying schools increases their skills. Perhaps if we scaled up whatever these high-flying schools are doing, we could reduce societal-level achievement gaps.

I'm all for figuring out what works well in schools and sharing that information, but we should be clear about what this approach to reducing achievement gaps means. The implicit assumption behind these studies is that disadvantaged children typically endure much worse learning environments than advantaged children, and that by exposing them to positive schools, the playing field is leveled. But as we learned in chapter 4, that's not the case. As schools are currently constituted, disadvantaged and advantaged children enjoy roughly similar opportunities to learn. So what do these studies demonstrate? They show that if you provide disadvantaged children with substantially *better* schooling than what they typically receive (or advantaged children typically receive) you can reduce achievement gaps.

The problem here should be obvious—seriously reducing societal-level achievement gaps via school reform would then require a national school system where disadvantaged children enjoy considerably better schools than advantaged children.

I don't mean that disadvantaged children just go to schools with a little more funding or slightly better teachers. They would have to go to schools about 1.5 times as good as the schools advantaged children attend for the schools to begin to make a dent in inequality.[8] The difference in quality would be so large that it would be obvious to everyone.

Some of us might be ok with redistributing school resources in this Robin Hood way, but this kind of school reform would be very challenging politically. Just trying to get the state of Ohio to distribute money *evenly* across schools has resulted in World War III–like battles since the 1990s. It's difficult to imagine voters supporting a system that provides considerably *more* resources to schools serving disadvantaged children. The problem is that schools are a highly salient feature of the state, and parents are reluctant to see this notable feature providing more for other people's children. Compensatory state programs are a dish best served cold. That means that people are likely more willing to redistribute if the consequences are not in their face every day. Adjusting tax codes, for example, is a subtler way of redistributing resources than school reform.

But even if we could pull off creating a society where disadvantaged children enjoy much better schools than advantaged children, would it be the best way to combat achievement gaps? Recall that the gaps are nearly entirely formed at kindergarten entry and so even though it may be possible to reduce gaps via school reform, it makes more sense to try and prevent large gaps from emerging in the first place. Consider this analogy Downey and Condron provided in a 2016 study:

> Marathon Runner A finishes an hour behind Runner B solely because Runner A started the race an hour late. Of course, in preparation for the next race, it would be possible for Runner A to close the gap by training harder to

run at a faster pace, but the most straightforward way to reduce the gap would be to start the race at the same time. Similarly, additional school reforms could reduce SES-based achievement gaps, but we recommend working toward more equal skills at the starting line. We say this because large SES-based gaps in cognitive skills emerge before kindergarten even begins, and these gaps do not grow appreciably as children progress through school.[9]

SO WHAT SHOULD WE DO?

If schools reflect more than generate inequality, and school reform is not the most efficient way to address the problem, what should we do? First, we need to make sure that when we hold schools accountable for their performance, it is for something that is under their control. The impact results from chapter 4 suggest that many of our value-added models designed to gauge school performance are probably underestimating the quality of teaching that occurs in schools serving children from disadvantaged backgrounds and overestimating the quality of what occurs in classrooms of advantaged children. Because we over-attribute outcomes observed in schools (like low test scores) to the teachers and administrators of those schools, we make it even less likely that people will want to work at those schools or send their children there.

Second, it means that when we observe different practices between schools, we should not necessarily assume that they are designed to perpetuate inequality. For example, if a school serving disadvantaged children funds fewer Advanced Placement classes than a school serving advantaged children, some scholars might interpret this as evidence of how schools provide different opportunities based on students' background. In one sense this is true. The disadvantaged child will end up with a different school experience (fewer opportunities for AP classes) than the advantaged child. But to describe the problem as one rooted in school inequality is not quite right. The administrators at the school serving disadvantaged children may simply be using their resources in the most productive way possible, which might mean that there is no Advanced Placement French class and more resources put toward remedial classes. In this way, the school is not so much generating inequality as responding to the inequality it receives in the most reasonable way. Inequality might be even worse if the school put its resources toward Advanced Placement French rather than remedial classes.

Third, thinking of schools as mostly reflectors prompts us to reconsider how racial and socioeconomic segregation matter. Perhaps if the public were more aware of how well each school really promotes learning, advantaged parents might be less inclined to concentrate their children in schools with children from other advantaged families. By contributing to the narrative that schools serving advantaged children are substantially better than schools serving the disadvantaged, The Assumption promotes further segregation of children across schools.[10]

This segregation likely matters. Children tend to perform better in school when surrounded by high-performing peers.[11] This makes sense because high-performing peers tend to value schoolwork more and are less likely to produce distractions with disruptive behavior. There may develop an "epidemic" in schools, where good or bad behavior is contagious, depending on the composition of students. And neighborhood researchers have demonstrated that concentrating disadvantaged families into one area tends to be bad for those families. The same is likely true when it comes to schools. Segregation is likely one of those school forces working to make inequality worse.

But again, this may be a case where we see a problem, in this case segregation, primarily through a school lens. School segregation is usually rooted in residential segregation. Where children attend school is primarily shaped by where they live and yet school-based segregation by income and race is too often addressed via school reforms. Busing poor urban children to suburban schools was one attempt to address this problem. Offering school choice to parents is another and drawing school districts in ways that encourage integration is yet another. But note that these school-based solutions would not be necessary if we didn't have such dramatic residential segregation in the first place. It's this segregation outside of schools that provides the larger context and determines the magnitude of the problem within schools.[12]

Some argue that residential segregation outside of schools is something we just have to live with. People prefer to live near people like themselves, the argument goes, and so we just have to deal with that reality. I disagree. Much housing segregation was deliberately created by governmental authorities—it did not just happen. The National Housing Act of 1934 instituted the policy of "redlining" areas with black families as poor loan risks, thereby facilitating racial residential segregation at the policy level. There are a wide range of policy decisions we can make that would encourage greater residential integration now, which would then lead to greater school integration. Heather Schwartz, in her report "Housing Policy Is School Policy," makes several suggestions. For example, we can require that when building a new subdivision, builders must create some low-income housing too.[13] This way we're less likely to produce another gated-like community of individuals largely divorced from the realities of the poor.

Finally, one could view this book's message as a major bummer—the problem of inequality is bigger and more difficult to address than we thought. That is an accurate read but I want to end with what I see as the silver lining. The value of this book is how it directs our attention more toward the root of the problem, the inequalities that have grown outside of schools during the last few decades, the ones that make it less likely for an individual to improve their position relative to their parents in the U.S. than in most other advanced countries. And we can and should reduce those.

One reason to focus outside of schools is that our current level of inequality isn't a result of fairness. We should reduce inequality because our growing prosperity hasn't been shared. In a fair society, when the whole country's wealth increases, everyone should be a little better off. But what we've experienced is that the gains in our economy over the last few decades have disproportionately accrued to those on top. For example, adjusted for inflation, the average income for households in the top 1 percent grew 118 percent between 1979 and 2016. For the bottom quintile, however, the rise was quite modest: just 33 percent.[14]

So, if we are to reduce inequality in broader society, what should we do? The simple answer is that we should expand the welfare state. I realize that by putting the word "welfare" in that sentence it will make some people cringe. They will immediately think of some lazy, undeserving slob collecting checks and avoiding work. But what I mean is more about reducing individual-level risk. In our modern economy everyone faces some risk: becoming sick, trying to develop employable skills, finding a job, enduring job loss, starting a family, and retiring. Each of these life events is tenuous and presents considerable uncertainty. For many these can be just short-term bumps in the road, but for some they can end up completely derailing a positive trajectory. We make a better society by reducing the individual-level risk during these events through many current programs (e.g., public schools, Medicaid, Medicare, Social Security), but the U.S reduces this risk considerably less than other rich countries do. I encourage us to do more.

Some scholars are optimistic that, eventually, we will do

more. In his article "America's Social Democratic Future," Lane Kenworthy explains why it is likely that we will eventually expand the role of government and reduce risk, especially for the most vulnerable:

> U.S. policymakers will recognize the benefits of a larger government role in pursuing economic security, equal opportunity, and rising living standards and will attempt to move the country in that direction. Often, they will fail. But sometimes, they will succeed. Progress will be incremental, coming in fits and starts, as it has in the past. New programs and expansions of existing ones will tend to persist, because programs that work well become popular and because the U.S. policymaking process makes it difficult for opponents of social programs to remove them. Small steps and the occasional big leap, coupled with limited backsliding, will have the cumulative effect of significantly increasing the breadth and generosity of government social programs.[15]

Although the current political climate in 2020 may not be amenable to a greater sharing of risk, Kenworthy's thesis is that the long arc of history is toward an expansion of the welfare state and a better life for most citizens. The U.S. will eventually move toward a system that shares more risk and is more consistent with the American Dream, he argues, because as nations become richer, they tend to become less comfortable with allowing some people to suffer (i.e., endure risk on their own). The U.S. is no exception; our total government spending on all programs as a percentage of GDP increased from 12 percent in 1920 to 37 percent in 2007.

I hope Kenworthy is right, that the most likely path is that the U.S. will expand the role of government to diminish risk for vulnerable individuals, thereby reducing inequality in broader society. This is the path that would put us more in line with how other rich countries treat their citizens. Of course, it is unlikely that this will be a linear path. There will be times when it may not look like we're headed down this path at all, like after President Trump signed the 2018 Tax Cuts and Jobs Act, legislation that likely increased inequality in several ways.

The struggle to create a better society, one consistent with American values of equal opportunity and fair treatment, will likely come as the result of many long-fought battles. How long those battles take will depend on whether we direct our resources effectively. For many scholars and policymakers, reducing inequality via school reform would be where they would direct much of their efforts. But their ideas are typically shaped by The Assumption, which is contradicted by key evidence. As we try to create a more just society, our efforts will be most productive if we start with a clear understanding of how schools matter.

ACKNOWLEDGMENTS

Three people deserve special praise for helping me write this book. My adviser in graduate school at Indiana University, Brian Powell, taught me the foundations of good social science research. From Brian, I learned to think hard about alternative explanations and explore them rigorously with data. Brian was a challenging adviser who constantly pushed me to think clearly and do more and better analysis. His research approach has led me to question others' narratives and wonder if the story changes if we develop a more comprehensive look at the evidence. Much of my career, including this book, has been built around making the case that existing narratives do not always hold up well to careful analysis. Brian recently received a prestigious mentoring award from the Spencer Foundation. It was a pleasure to see him honored this way because he makes such significant investments in his students. It's been twenty-eight years since I earned my Ph.D. under his supervision, but I still owe a lot to his training.

Second, my frequent coauthor, Paul von Hippel, also merits praise. In one of the more awkward professional relationships of my career, Paul was my advisee while he earned a Ph.D. in sociology at Ohio State. I describe this relationship as awkward because Paul taught me way more than I taught him, a fact obvious to both of us but Paul was too nice to ever say out loud. Paul is an especially talented statistician, and he has created modeling approaches that set the standard for seasonal comparisons. He has also made significant contributions to the theoretical understanding of schools and inequality. It was Paul, for example, who realized that studying how overall variance in skills changes across seasons provides a more comprehensive test of how schools influence inequality than monitoring socioeconomic or racial/ethnic gaps. What I admire the most about Paul is his willingness to change his mind about how the world works if the data are strong. He is intellectually rigorous and flexible—a rare combination.

Finally, my wife Mo has also helped make this project better. Perhaps a brief story will explain. A few years ago we were at a party in Gambier, Ohio, when a topic of conversation piqued my interest. The group I was in started debating the best way to drive to Columbus—229 or 36. Since I have commuted to Ohio State for years, I happily explained my data collection procedures, the variables I measured, and my conclusion—229 is about thirty seconds faster (except on Fridays when it's more like one minute faster). That is very interesting, Doug, thank you for carefully collecting such useful data, we appreciate this information: these were all things that no one said. Instead, the group stared at their shoes and the topic shifted. People don't want to hear about your Excel spreadsheet, Mo explained to me in the car on the way home. They like driving to Columbus a certain way (229 or 36), and they aren't really interested in your data. I thought about that for a long time, and it is part of why this book has a part 2. At first all I wanted to talk about was part 1—the evidence—but Mo has helped me understand that there is a reason why people are resistant to evidence, and it's worth thinking about that.

I would also like to thank the Center for Advanced Study in the Behavioral Sciences at Stanford University. I spent a 2017–18 sabbatical year at this academic heaven and I initiated the work on this book. At lunch one day, the director of the center, Margaret Levi, encouraged me to get my ideas out there and engage a broader audience. That's the goal of this book. I'm also grateful to Radboud University. Their sociology department invited me to the Netherlands for a few months in 2019, and I finished the book while enjoying its excellent intellectual environment. I'm grateful to Herbert Kraaycamp and Margriet van Hek for hosting me.

I'm also thankful for several funding organizations that sponsored research reported in this book: Spencer Foundation, William T. Grant Foundation, and the Sage Foundation. And I'm grateful for the feedback I've received from several universities and organizations where I presented these ideas. These include: Radboud University 2019; Stanford University 2018; Notre Dame 2018; the Scandinavian Consortium for Organizational Research 2018; WZB Berlin Social Science Center 2017; the Crane Center for Early Childhood Research and Policy 2017; Indiana University 2016; Yale University 2016; Oxford University 2015; Duke University 2015; New York University 2014; Johns Hopkins University 2013; Harvard University 2013; University of Virginia 2012; Penn State University 2012; Yale University 2011; Emory University 2010; McMaster University 2009; University of Minnesota 2008; Florida State University 2008.

APPENDIX A

The Early Childhood Longitudinal Datasets (ECLS-K:1998 and ECLS-K:2010)

The Early Childhood Longitudinal Study, Kindergarten Cohort of 1988 (ECLS-K:1998). Collected by the National Center for Education Statistics, the ECLS-K:1998 provides information for a nationally representative sample of 21,260 children attending kindergarten in the fall of 1998–1999. The ECLS-K employed a multistage probability sampling design in which 100 Primary Sampling Units (PSUs) (counties or groups of counties) were selected with probability proportional to size, and then roughly 1,200 schools were sampled, and about 24 students within each school were selected. Children were assessed by teachers at the beginning and end of kindergarten, end of first grade, spring of third grade, and spring of fifth grade. What makes the data so valuable for seasonal comparison researchers is that a random sample of roughly 3,500 students were assessed in the fall of first grade, allowing for estimates of summer learning between kindergarten and first grade.

The Early Childhood Longitudinal Study, Kindergarten Cohort of 2010 (ECLS-K:2010).[1] The ECLS-K 2010 data is a nationally-representative sample of 16,450 students who were enrolled in kindergarten in the fall of 2010. Again, ECLS-K used a multistage probability sampling design in which primary sampling units (PSUs) were sampled, then roughly 1,000 schools were sampled within PSUs, and about 19 students within each school were selected. Children's were observed in the fall and spring of kindergarten and the fall and spring of first grade. In first and second grade, fall tests were given to a 30 percent subsample of participating students, allowing for estimates of summer learning after kindergarten and after first grade. The ECLS-K:2010 also observed children in the spring of third, fourth, and fifth grades, but these newer observations did not include commensurate fall observations and so do not allow for separate estimates of school and summer learning.

APPENDIX B

Limitations of Seasonal
Comparison Studies

Like all empirical methods, seasonal comparison research requires assumptions. One assumption is that gains made at the bottom of a scale of some cognitive skill (e.g., reading or math) mean the same thing as gains made near the top. As I mentioned in chapter 4, if it is easier to produce gains among children beginning with initially low skills, then perhaps the seasonal results do not suggest that schools serving disadvantaged children are doing better than most think. It may be that schools serving disadvantaged children really are substantially poorer learning environments and yet they don't look that way from seasonal studies because it is just easier to produce learning gains for children beginning low on a scale. This concern is also consistent with the generally observed pattern that children learn fastest at the younger ages (e.g., kindergarten through third grade) and that their learning rate tends to level off at later stages of schooling.

The solution to this problem is to use interval-level scales where a unit increase at the bottom of the scale represents the same thing as a unit increase at the top. But while psychometricians try to produce scales with interval-like characteristics, it's difficult to know how well they succeed. To complicate the issue further, Ballou (2008) makes the point that scales can be interval with respect to one construct but not another. For example, it could be that a scale that is interval with respect to the latent ability construct but not interval with respect to the amount of effort required by a student or teacher to make a particular amount of gain. So, both things could be true—that the scale is interval with respect to latent math or reading skills, but it is nevertheless easier for teachers to promote gains with students who start out at lower levels. I know of no way to test this possibility, however.

Given these issues, should we worry that the seasonal comparison results overestimate the school-based learning produced by schools serving disadvantaged children (typically starting lower on cognitive skill scales)? While I think this is an issue that should be debated further among scholars, I do not think this concern is enough to dismiss the seasonal patterns. One of the strengths of seasonal comparison research is its *comparison* across seasons. If it really is easier to make gains when starting at the bottom of a scale, then it should be easier to make them both during the school and summer seasons. We can't just selectively apply our concern about the scale to the period when children are in school and then pretend that it doesn't matter during the summers. Of course, even if the problem applies equally to both seasons, it still might bias our view of how schools matter because the school period is longer. For this reason, David Quinn, Melissa Alcaraz, and I have estimated school "impact" (discussed in chapter 4) with models adjusting for children's starting point at kindergarten entry (see Downey, Quinn, and Alcaraz 2019 for details). These models test whether we would see greater evidence of school-based learning in schools typically serving advantaged kids if we accounted for the fact that they typically serve more children who begin with stronger skills. Our results indicated that we would not and that our main patterns were robust—compared to schools serving advantaged children, schools serving disadvantaged children produced similar levels of school-based learning net of children's starting point on a math or reading scale.

One can also circumvent this problem by avoiding the assumption that the scale is interval and simply asking, does a group's relative position improve more when school is in versus not? To date, my colleagues and I have consistently produced the same overall patterns when we have employed this nonparametric approach.

Another assumption in a crossover research design is that there is no spillover between treatment and control periods. For our purposes that means that the seasonal design allows us to cleanly separate school from nonschool influences. That is nearly an impossible task given the complex interrelationship between the two, and so seasonal studies only provide an estimate of how schools matter, assuming a clean demarcation. That clean distinction is unlikely for many reasons. Imagine estimating the effect of a drug by comparing treatment and control periods, but the drug ended up staying in the patient's system for so long that it was affecting observations well into the control part of the study. For seasonal comparison studies, we need to assume that there is little spillover across seasons. This kind of contamination could occur, for example, if schools influence children's summer learning through school-sponsored reading programs. To the extent that schools are influencing summer learning, the seasonal comparison method fails to isolate school effects.

In addition, children are sometimes influenced by schools prior to kindergarten or via summer school programs, both of which undermine the notion that these are nonschool periods. There is not much that can be done about this complication, and so it forces us to acknowledge that scores at kindergarten entry do not necessarily represent nonschool environments alone.

What we can say is that children's skills have not yet been influenced by our K-12 system of public education. Attending summer school also complicates seasonal models because it contaminates estimates of learning independent of schooling. For that reason, the seasonal studies I've relied on most heavily in this book exclude children who attended summer school.

It is also difficult to know the extent to which schools influence summer learning even for children who do not attend summer school. In our own studies, we have been able to assess it at some level because we had information about whether a school sent children home with a booklist or summer reading program. While these are limited indicators, it is noteworthy that they were uncorrelated with children's summer learning. To date, therefore, the evidence suggests that this assumption is reasonable.

Related to this spillover problem is a practical issue. Students are virtually never tested on the first and last days of school and so when we estimate summer learning by comparing test scores from fall and spring, there is almost always overlap of days of school contaminating the estimate. For example, in the ECLS-K:1998 data children were, on average, assessed on October 10 in the fall and on April 4 in the spring. Average school years start in late August and end in early June, meaning that any estimate of summer learning between a spring and fall assessment would be influenced not just by the summer, but also by about fifteen weeks of schooling—seven to eight on each side of the summer. Seasonal comparison scholars try to reduce the extent of this problem by modeling the school segments of learning and subtracting them from estimates of summer learning, but it's difficult to know whether this modeling approach resolves the problem adequately.

Finally, we want to know the causal effect of schooling on inequality in cognitive skills, but it is hard to know what inequality would look like if children experienced less (or more) school. The logic behind seasonal comparisons is that the summer patterns provide a window into what happens when children are not in school, but it's unclear that what we observe in the summers would inform what would happen if we expanded the school year so that kids went to school longer, say 220 days a year rather than 180. Do the patterns we observe in the summer really provide a window into that counterfactual? They do unless parents would change their behavior considerably if they knew their children were going to attend school so much more. If a school increased its calendar in this way and then high-SES parents also increased their nonschool investments (and low-SES parents did not), the change could increase inequality in skills much more than current seasonal patterns suggest.

APPENDIX C
How Should Social Scientists Study Schools and Inequality?

This book is primarily aimed at a general audience, but hopefully it will also prompt scholars to reconsider their approach to studying schools and inequality. Here are my recommendations.

(1) We need to take more seriously the challenge of identifying how schools matter when children's outcomes are shaped by both school and nonschool factors. Children spend most of their waking hours outside of school (87 percent) and good research addresses this confound rigorously. Traditional scholarship attempting to isolate school effects by statistically controlling for children's nonschool environments is not up to the task because the vast majority of why some children learn faster than others is not captured by typically available indicators in survey data.

(2) Experimental studies are well-suited for isolating school effects because they employ random assignment. But these studies tend to ask the question, "Are some school processes better at promoting learning than others?" The answer, unremarkably, is yes. This approach tells us little about the bigger question: How does school exposure affect inequality?

(3) Nonexperimental studies that attempt to understand how schools matter by only observing what happens when school is in session are poorly suited for the task. Just as it is hard to determine the effect of a treatment without comparing it to the nontreatment period, it is similarly difficult to know how schools matter without comparing observations made during school and nonschool periods.

(4) There exist both school processes that increase and decrease inequality. If we primarily study those that increase inequality, we will end up with a distorted picture of schools. While there is value in asking, "Is there anything going on in schools that increases inequality?" the answer is almost surely "yes." That doesn't tell us much, however, about schools' overall effect on inequality because countervailing compensatory forces might also be operating.

(5) If The Assumption is wrong, there are many important questions that require attention from scholars with a contextual perspective. Why are achievement gaps so large at kindergarten entry? How are these gaps changing over time and why? Why do they vary among countries? What are the primary characteristics of broader society that generate large inequalities in cognitive skills prior to formal schooling? How is it that schools serving disadvantaged children manage to produce as much school-based learning as schools serving advantaged children? What are the primary school characteristics that reduce inequality? This is the perfect job for sociologists, and yet surprisingly little research has addressed these questions.

NOTES

INTRODUCTION

1. Entwisle and Alexander 1992.
2. Kozol 1991.
3. The film was produced in 1995 and so, assumedly, more schools have access to computers now.
4. Downey, von Hippel, and Broh 2004.
5. Downey, von Hippel, and Hughes 2008.
6. Schneider 2018: xvii.
7. Ballantine, Spade, and Stuber 2017.
8. Coleman et al. 1966; Jencks et al. 1972. Also see Tyack and Cuban 1995 and Berliner and Biddle 1996. Both made the case that the notion that American's schools were in dire need of reform was overblown.
9. Fischer et al. 1996.
10. Depending on what our social comparison is (e.g., parents' socioeconomic status, income, education), math gaps sometimes narrow over time.
11. Alexander 1997: 16.
12. Cornman et al. 2017.
13. Fischer et al. 1996.
14. Condron 2011.

CHAPTER 1

1. Walberg 1984:397.
2. Nicholas attended half-day kindergarten, and so he will have spent 12.5 years in school at 180 days each year; that's 2,250 days. At 6.5 hours a day, that's 14,625 hours of school by age 18. If we allow him to sleep 10 hours a day, that means that when he's 18, he's been awake for 14 (hours a day) × 18 (years) × 365 (days) = 91,980 hours. 14,625/91,980 = 15.9 percent. This estimate will be high because it does not account for school closings (e.g., snow days) or sick days. Of course, the estimate is higher if children attend preschool.

CHAPTER 2

1. The reading scale used by ECLS-K employs modern psycho-metric practices and provides a good look at how the SES gaps change over time. Theta scores, plotted in figure 2.1, are estimates of the student's ability based on their answers to a set of items. Each item has a difficulty level and a student's probability of responding correctly to an item is modeled by the item response function, which is a function of student ability, item difficulty, and possibly other parameters.
2. Reardon 2011: figure 5.5.
3. Again, the pattern is not quite as strong in the Northwest Evaluation Association MAP scales, where overall variation tends to increase somewhat from kindergarten to eighth grade. Of course, that pattern by itself does not implicate schools because the increase could occur either for school or nonschool reasons.
4. For a discussion of the limitations of the Thurstone scale and how it likely distorted our understanding of schools' influence on achievement gaps, see von Hippel and Hamrock 2019. The Thurstone scale changed test forms across years, and scholars analyzed unstandardized scores uncorrected for measurement error (von Hippel and Hamrock 2019).
5. Recent research testing the equal-interval properties of the Measure of Academic Progress Growth scale from the Northwest Evaluation Association (an IRT scale similar to the one used in the ECLS-K) using additive conjoint modeling found strong support for the vertical scale (Thum 2018).
6. Reardon 2011.
7. Merry 2013.
8. Sopolsky 2017.
9. Hair et al. 2015.
10. Shonkoff and Garner (2012: e236) have reported that toxic stress experienced on a chronic basis "is associated with hypertrophy and overactivity in the amygdala and orbitofrontal cortex, whereas comparable levels of adversity can lead to loss of neurons and neural connections in the hippocampus and medial PFC [prefrontal cortex]."
11. Institute of Medicine and National Research Council 2000.
12. Sampson, Sharkey, and Raudenbush 2008.
13. Sopolsky 2017.
14. And it turns out that inequality in general is related to bad be-

havior among humans. For example, there is a .62 correlation between the level of income inequality in a country and the level of bullying. So, in the high-inequality U.S., 9 percent of kids admit that they have bullied someone two or more times in the past couple of months. In contrast, in low-inequality Denmark the bullying is less than half that, at 4 percent (Due et al. 2009).

15. Corak 2013.

CHAPTER 3

1. Burkam et al. 2004.
2. Downey, Quinn, and Alcaraz 2019.
3. Firebaugh 2008; Gangl 2010.
4. See Heyns 1978: tables 3.1–2. Whites gain on blacks faster when school is out (summers) than when it is in, especially in the seventh-grade sample.
5. See von Hippel, Workman, and Downey 2018; Quinn et al. 2016.
6. The negative effect of school exposure on the black/white gap is complex for several reasons. First, it is typically evident only when comparing black and white students of the same SES. Because lower-SES children typically benefit more from school exposure than high-SES children, disadvantaged black children experience countervailing forces. Second, it is evident at the individual level, and yet, as chapter 4 explains, children's school-based learning is no different, on average, in schools serving mostly white versus mostly black students.
7. Von Hippel, Workman, and Downey 2018.
8. Downey, von Hippel, and Broh 2004.
9. Von Hippel, Workman, and Downey 2018.
10. See von Hippel and Hamrock (2019, table 3, ECLS-K ability, unstandardized coefficients). The standardized coefficients may not be appropriate here because they do not allow the variance to change over time, which is most likely not realistic. Von Hippel and Hamrock also note that the Growth Research Database from the NWEA suggests that the black/white gap grows more—by nearly half in math and three-quarters in reading—and that it is unclear why the two datasets produce different estimates.

CHAPTER 4

1. Downey, von Hippel, and Hughes 2008.
2. Recall that the average American eighteen-year-old has spent 87

percent of their waking hours outside of school. For any calendar year during the school years, that figure is about 75 percent. The overall estimate (87 percent) is higher because most children spend little of their prekindergarten years in school.

3. So, are the reading and math scales used by seasonal comparison researchers created this way so that increases at the bottom mean the same as increases near the top? At first, they were not. As mentioned earlier, the famous Baltimore study relied on Thurstone scaling that had multiple problems. For example, they would follow children for several years of schooling but change forms of the test as the children aged. So, children might take one type of test at the end of third grade and then a different kind when they returned in the fall for fourth grade. Changing test forms in this way may have inflated what looked like "summer loss" simply because children were less familiar with the new testing format in the fall.

   Our first seasonal study also used a suboptimal scale. Several years after publication, we learned that these scales were probably not interval level, partly because there were not equal numbers of easy, medium, and tough questions. The National Center for Education Statistics then produced new scales that were more carefully designed to gauge children's ability (theta) in an interval manner. Once the theta scales were released, we immediately reevaluated our previous work, aware that it might have been wrong if the seasonal patterns depended heavily on this scaling issue. It turned out that the patterns we originally found using the poorer scale didn't change much with the better theta scale.

4. I wouldn't want to evaluate schools via impact for the long term for another reason. As soon as you start doing that then schools have an incentive for their children not to learn anything during the summers.

5. Jencks and Phillips 1998.

6. Jencks and Phillips 1998: 3–4.

7. I've seen this occur at Kenyon College, where my wife works as a counselor for students headed to medical school. Maureen has developed relationships with several of the deans at Ohio medical schools. Every few years she has a strong student who is not getting accepted anywhere, which prompts her to phone her long-time contacts in admissions and go to bat for the student. It almost always works.

8. Boyd et al. 2005.

9. Gordon, Kane, and Staiger 2006.
10. Chetty, Friedman, and Rockoff 2014: 2595, and appendix D.
11. Downey, Quinn, and Alcaraz 2019. We were also able to improve on the 2008 study by employing theta ability scales and following children for a longer period of time.
12. Isenberg et al. 2016.
13. Lareau and Goyette 2014.

PART II

1. Coleman et al. 1966: 325.
2. Not everyone agrees with me that more modern methods lead to a position that schools play a more compensatory role than what Coleman thought. For example, Borman and Dowling (2010) reanalyzed the Equality of Educational Opportunity Data, which Coleman analyzed. With more sophisticated multilevel models, they concluded that differences between schools matter *more* than Coleman concluded—they found that up to 40 percent of the variation in verbal skills was between schools. This seems to suggest that differences between schools matter a lot. But recall from chapter 2 that children's skills vary across schools in dramatic ways at kindergarten entry simply because different children attend different schools. Borman and Dowling attempted to address this issue by statistically controlling for some of the differences between children, but there is reason to believe that their indicators of family background (urbanism, parents' education, family structure, number of siblings, family resources, and reading material) do not fully capture all of the differences between families and so do not produce an unbiased estimate of school effects. As I argued in chapter 2, statistically equalizing the different children that attend different schools is unlikely to tell us how schools matter because most of these differences are not well captured by typical survey data. My view is that the seasonal comparison studies are better equipped for identifying schools' role than analysis of data collected at one point in time.

CHAPTER 5

1. Bowles and Gintis 1976; Anyon 1981.
2. Gershenson et al. 2018. See also Joshi, Doan, and Springer 2018.
3. Gregory, Skiba, and Noguera 2010.
4. National Center for Education Statistics 2012.
5. These numbers can be generated from the Ohio Department of Education website. See http://education.ohio.gov/Topics

/Finance-and-Funding/Finance-Related-Data/Expenditure
-and-Revenue/Expenditure-Revenue-Data.
6. The differences in "instructional expenditures" are somewhat greater. For example, instructional expenditures for the Columbus school district were less ($7,173) than for Upper Arlington ($9,689), Bexley ($8,442), and Worthington ($7,673) in 2011–12. Even when the comparison is restricted to instructional expenditures, however, the differences are more modest than many expect.
7. Isenberg et al., 2016; Chetty, Friedman, and Rockoff 2014.
8. Merry 2013.
9. Zuberi 2006.
10. Reardon 2011.
11. Goyette 2008; Renzulli and Roscigno 2005.
12. Rothstein 2004.
13. Green and Benner 2018.
14. Dobbie and Fryer 2011.
15. Hassrick, Raudenbush, and Rosen 2017.
16. Hassrick, Raudenbush, and Rosen 2017.
17. Duncan and Murnane 2014.
18. Heckman and Masterov 2007.
19. Heckman and Masterov 2007.
20. Farkas and Beron 2004.
21. Whitehurst 2016.

CHAPTER 6

1. Von Hippel 2010.
2. Kozol 1991.
3. National Center for Education Statistics 2010.
4. Corcoran et al. 2004.
5. Collins and Hoxie 2017.
6. Piketty 2014.
7. Von Hippel 2010.
8. Millard and Aragon 2015; National Association for Gifted Children 2015.
9. Bourdieu 1977.
10. DiMaggio 1982.
11. Kingston 2001.
12. Duffett, Farkas, and Loveless 2008.
13. Anyon 1981.
14. Downey, Workman, and von Hippel 2019.
15. Von Hippel et al. 2007; von Hippel and Workman 2016.

CHAPTER 7

1. Specia 2017.
2. Freedman 2007.
3. Medina 2010.
4. Ropeik 2010.
5. We like to think that this comes from our strong individualistic values. It is popular to believe that Americans are more likely to value choices that conflict with the larger group, challenge authority, and prioritize personal liberty. When the Nazis defended themselves at the Nuremburg trials with the position that they were just following orders, Americans scoffed, confident that they would not have just sent people to the gas chambers because of orders. Americans are more willing to defy authority, we like to think. But it's not clear that they really are. If we ask people, "In general, would you say that people should obey the law without exception, or are there exceptional occasions on which people should follow their consciences even if it means breaking the law?" and compare across countries, most Americans would expect that we would stand out as one of the most likely nations to respond in favor of conscience over law. But we're not. About 45 percent of Americans favor conscience, compared to 50 percent of Danes, 52 percent of Norwegians, 58 percent of Brits, 61 percent of Germans, 65 percent of Dutch and Finns, 68 percent of Swedes, and 78 percent of French. Americans are exceptional but in the opposite way most would predict. And this isn't just a weird question, we get the same results if we gauge responses to "People should support their country even if the country is in the wrong." So, this kind of individualism is not the kind where America is exceptional. Instead, Americans stand out in terms of their hostility to government and social programs. It's more about being antigovernment than about liberty. Fischer 2010.
6. Kantor and Lowe 2013.
7. Steffes 2012: 207.
8. Katz 2013; McCall 2013.
9. Moynihan, Rainwater, and Yancey 1967: 12.
10. Ryan 1971.
11. Massey and Sampson 2009: 12.
12. Massey 1995: 747–48.
13. Herrnstein and Murray 1994.
14. National Center for Education Statistics 2017.

15. Levanon, England, and Allison 2009.
16. There is a famous paper written in 1981 by Eric Hanushek titled "Throwing Money at Schools," where he argued that "there is no relationship between expenditures and the achievement of students." Hanushek noted the very modest correlations between school investments and children's outcomes and questioned traditional approaches to school reform, such as reducing class size or trying to hire better-trained teachers. He concluded that there's little to be gained by just investing more money in schools. But his solution was still school-based—he recommended that we focus on restructuring schools to create the proper incentives for a better learning environment. Even though the data were telling him that school characteristics didn't matter much, he couldn't escape the school-centric world of solutions.

CHAPTER 8

1. Fletcher and Tienda 2009.
2. More recent analyses suggest that they may have given up too soon. For example, Schneider (2016) reports that small schools improved graduation rates by 9.5 percent, a pretty large outcome.
3. Russakoff 2015.
4. Kotlowitz 2015.
5. Ohio Department of Education 2019.
6. Rawls 1999.
7. One challenge to implementing an impact measure of accountability is that over time it could incentivize schools to reduce summer learning (they would be evaluated on the difference between school and summer learning rates). In addition, schooling is about more than just raising math and reading test scores. When we narrow our evaluations to these kinds of test scores, we necessarily narrow the curriculum.
8. I employ this 1.5 times estimate from the fact that successful high-flying schools tend to expose their children to about 1.5 times more schooling than traditional schools.
9. Downey and Condron 2016b: 235.
10. One school-based solution is to redistribute school days across the entire year and avoid the long summer, when disadvantaged children often fall behind. Paul von Hippel studied how inequality plays out in schools that employ year-round rather than traditional school calendars. He concludes that, once the dust clears,

achievement gaps operate in much the same way in year-round schools—although SES-based gaps don't form over a long summer, they form in little bits during the smaller breaks (von Hippel 2016). In short, we can't change achievement gaps much just by redistributing the days of school more evenly across the calendar. The seasonal patterns do suggest, however, that more exposure to schooling would work in the direction of reducing inequality. That means that if the number of days children attended school were increased from 180 to say, 220, we would expect this kind of policy to help reduce SES-based achievement gaps while potentially increasing black/white ones. The overall effect would be modest, however, given that the gaps change little during the school years.

11. Ewijk and Sleegers 2010.
12. Rothstein 2004.
13. Schwartz 2010.
14. Congressional Budget Office 2019.
15. Kenworthy 2014: 90.

APPENDIX A

1. Some refer to these data as ECLS-K:2011 but we refer to it as the 2010 data because that is when children were first observed, similar to the 1998 cohort.

REFERENCES

Alexander, Karl L. 1997. "Public Schools and the Public Good." *Social Forces* 76 (1): 1–30.

Anyon, Jean. 1981. "Social Class and School Knowledge." *Curriculum Inquiry* 11 (1): 3.

Ballantine, Jeanne H., Joan Z. Spade, and Jenny Stuber. 2017. *Schools and Society: A Sociological Approach to Education*. 6th ed. Los Angeles, CA: Pine Forge Press.

Ballou, Dale. 2008. "Test Scaling and Value-Added Measurement." Paper presented at the Wisconsin Center for Education Research's National Conference on Value-Added Modeling. https://eric.ed.gov/?id=ED510378.

Berliner, David C., and Bruce J. (Bruce Jesse) Biddle. 1996. *The Manufactured Crisis: Myths, Fraud, and the Attack on America's Public Schools*. Addison-Wesley.

Borman, Geoffrey, and Maritza Dowling. 2010. "Schools and Inequality: A Multilevel Analysis of Coleman's Equality of Educational Opportunity Data." *Teachers College Record* 112 (5): 1201–46.

Bourdieu, Pierre. 1977. "Cultural Reproduction and Social Reproduction." In *Power and Ideology in Education*, edited by J. Karabel and A. H. Halsey, 487–511. New York: Oxford University.

Bowles, Samuel, and Herbert Gintis. 1976. *Schooling in Capitalist America: Educational Reform and the Contradictions of Economic Life*. New York: Basic Books.

Boyd, Donald, Hamilton Lankford, Susanna Loeb, and James Wyckoff. 2005. "Explaining the Short Careers of High-Achieving Teachers in Schools with Low-Performing Students." *American Economic Review* 95 (2): 166–71.

Burkam, David T., Douglas D. Ready, Valerie E. Lee, and Laura F. LoGerfo. 2004. "Social-Class Differences in Summer Learning between Kindergarten and First Grade: Model Specification and Estimation." *Sociology of Education* 77 (1): 1–31.

Chetty, Raj, John N. Friedman, and Jonah E. Rockoff. 2014. "Measuring the Impacts of Teachers II: Teacher Value-Added and Student

Outcomes in Adulthood." *American Economic Review* 104 (9): 2633–79.

Coleman, James S., Ernest Q. Campbell, Carol J. Hobson, James McPartland, Alexander M. Mood, Frederic D. Weinfeld, and Robert L. York. 1966. *Equality of Educational Opportunity.* Washington: Government Printing Office.

Collins, Chuck, and Josh Hoxie. 2017. *Billionaire Bonanza: The Forbes 400 and the Rest of Us.* Washington, DC: Institute for Policy Studies.

Condron, Dennis. 2011. "Egalitarianism and Educational Excellence: Compatible Goals for Affluent Societies?" *Educational Researcher* 40 (2): 47–55.

Congressional Budget Office. 2019. *The Distribution of Household Income, 2016.* Washington D. C.

Corak, Miles. 2013. "Income Inequality, Equality of Opportunity, and Intergenerational Mobility." *Journal of Economic Perspectives* 27 (3): 79–102.

Corcoran, Sean P., William N. Evans, Jennifer Godwin, Sheila E. Murray, and Robert M. Schwab. 2004. "The Changing Distribution of Education Finance, 1972–1997." In *Social Inequality*, edited by K. M. Neckerman. New York, NY: Russell Sage Foundation.

Cornman, S. Q., Lei Zhou, M. R. Howell, and J. Young. 2017. *Revenues and Expenditures for Public Elementary and Secondary Education: School Year 2014–2015 (Fiscal Year 2015).* Washington, DC: U.S. Department of Education.

DiMaggio, Paul. 1982. "Cultural Capital and School Success: The Impact of Status Culture Participation on the Grades of U.S. High School Students." *American Sociological Review* 47 (2): 189–201.

Dobbie, Will, and Roland G. Fryer. 2011. "Are High Quality Schools Enough to Close the Achievement Gap? Evidence from a Social Experiment in Harlem." *American Economic Journal: Applied Economics* 3 (3): 158–87.

Downey, Douglas B., and D. J. Condron. 2016a. "Fifty Years since the Coleman Report: Rethinking the Relationship between Schools and Inequality." *Sociology of Education* 89 (3): 207–20.

Downey, Douglas B., and Dennis J. Condron. 2016b. "Two Questions for Sociologists of Education: A Rejoinder." *Sociology of Education* 89 (3): 234–35.

Downey, Douglas B., David Quinn, and Melissa Alcaraz. 2019. "The Distribution of School Quality." *Sociology of Education* 92 (4): 386–403.

Downey, Douglas B., Paul T. von Hippel, and Beckett A. Broh. 2004.

"Are Schools the Great Equalizer? Cognitive Inequality during the Summer Months and the School Year." *American Sociological Review* 69 (5): 613–35.

Downey, D. B., P. T. von Hippel, and M. Hughes. 2008. "Are 'Failing' Schools Really Failing? Using Seasonal Comparison to Evaluate School Effectiveness." *Sociology of Education* 81 (3): 242–70.

Downey, Douglas B., Joseph Workman, and Paul von Hippel. 2019. "Socioeconomic, Ethnic, Racial, and Gender Gaps in Children's Social/Behavioral Skills: Do They Grow Faster in School or Out?" *Sociological Science* 6: 446–66.

Due, Pernille, Juan Merlo, Yossi Harel-Fisch, Mogens Trab Damsgaard, Bjørn E. Holstein, Jørn Hetland, Candace Currie, Saoirse Nic Gabhainn, Margarida Gaspar De Matos, and John Lynch. 2009. "Socioeconomic Inequality in Exposure to Bullying during Adolescence: A Comparative, Cross-Sectional, Multilevel Study in 35 Countries." *American Journal of Public Health* 99 (5): 907–14.

Duffett, Ann, Steve Farkas, and Tom Loveless. 2008. *High-Achieving Students in the Era of No Child Left Behind.* Thomas B. Fordham Institute: Washington, DC.

Duncan, Greg J., and Richard J. Murnane. 2014. *Restoring Opportunity: The Crisis of Inequality and the Challenge for American Education.* Cambridge, MA: Harvard Education Press.

Entwisle, Doris R., and Karl L. Alexander. 1992. "Summer Setback: Race, Poverty, School Composition, and Mathematics Achievement in the First Two Years of School." *American Sociological Review* 57 (1): 72–84.

Ewijk, Reyn van, and Peter Sleegers. 2010. "The Effect of Peer Socioeconomic Status on Student Achievement: A Meta-Analysis." *Educational Research Review* 5 (2): 134–50.

Farkas, George, and Kurt Beron. 2004. "The Detailed Age Trajectory of Oral Vocabulary Knowledge: Differences by Class and Race." *Social Science Research* 33 (3): 464–97.

Firebaugh, Glenn. 2008. *Seven Rules for Social Research.* Princeton: Princeton University Press.

Fischer, Claude S. 2010. "Americans Not the Individuals We Think We Are." *The Dallas Morning News,* July 1.

Fischer, Claude S., Michael Hout, Martin Sanchez Jankowski, Samuel R. Lucas, Ann Swidler, and Kim Voss. 1996. *Inequality by Design: Cracking the Bell Curve Myth.* 1st ed. Princeton: Princeton University Press.

Fletcher, Jason M., and Marta Tienda. 2009. "High School Classmates and College Success." *Sociology of Education* 82 (4): 287–314.

Freedman, Samuel G. 2007. "Where Teachers Sit, Awaiting Their Fates." *New York Times*. Retrieved January 21, 2020. https://www.nytimes.com/2007/10/10/education/10education.html?searchResultPosition=3.

Fryer, Roland G., and Steven D. Levitt. 2004. "Understanding the Black-White Test Score Gap in the First Two Years of School." *The Review of Economics and Statistics* 86 (2): 447–64.

Gangl, Markus. 2010. "Causal Inference in Sociological Research." *Annual Review of Sociology* 36: 21–47.

Gershenson, Seth, Cassandra M. Hart, Joshua Hyman, Constance Lindsay, and Nicholas Papageorge. 2018. "The Long-Run Impacts of Same-Race Teachers." National Bureau of Economic Research, Working Paper Number 25254.

Gordon, Robert, Thomas J. Kane, and Douglas O. Staiger. 2006. *Identifying Effective Teachers Using Performance on the Job: The Hamilton Project, Discussion Paper 2006–01*. Washington, DC: Brookings Institution.

Goyette, Kimberly A. 2008. "Race, Social Background, and School Choice Options." *Equity & Excellence in Education* 41 (1): 114–29.

Green, Erica L., and Katie Benner. 2018. "Louisiana School Made Headlines for Sending Black Kids to Elite Colleges. Here's the Reality." *New York Times*, November 30.

Gregory, Anne, Russell J. Skiba, and Pedro A. Noguera. 2010. "The Achievement Gap and the Discipline Gap." *Educational Researcher* 39 (1): 59–68.

Hair, Nicole L., Jamie L. Hanson, Barbara L. Wolfe, and Seth D. Pollak. 2015. "Association of Child Poverty, Brain Development, and Academic Achievement." *JAMA Pediatrics* 169 (9): 822.

Hanushek, Eric A. 1981. "Throwing Money at Schools." *Journal of Policy Analysis and Management* 1 (1): 19–41.

Hassrick, Elizabeth McGhee, Stephen W. Raudenbush, and Lisa Stefanie Rosen. 2017. *The Ambitious Elementary School: Its Conception, Design, and Implications for Educational Equality*. Chicago, IL: University of Chicago Press.

Heckman, James J. 2006. "Skill Formation and the Economics of Investing in Disadvantaged Children." *Science* 312 (5782): 1900–1902.

Heckman, James J., and Dimitriy V. Masterov. 2007. "The Productivity Argument for Investing in Young Children." *Applied Economic Perspectives and Policy* 29 (3): 446–93.

Heckman, James J., Jora Stixrud, and Sergio Urzua. 2006. "The Effects of Cognitive and Noncognitive Abilities on Labor Market Outcomes and Social Behavior." *Journal of Labor Economics* 24 (3): 411–82.

Herrnstein, Richard J., and Charles Murray. 1994. *Bell Curve: Intelligence and Class Structure in American Life.* New York, NY: Free Press.

Institute of Medicine and National Research Council. 2000. *From Neurons to Neighborhoods: The Science of Early Childhood Development.* Washington, DC: National Academy Press.

Isenberg, Eric, Jeffrey Max, Philip Gleason, Matthew Johnson, Jonah Deutsch, and Michael Hansen. 2016. *Do Low-Income Students Have Equal Access to Effective Teachers? Evidence from 26 Districts (NCEE 2017-4008).* Washington, DC: National Center for Education Evaluation and Regional Assistance.

Jencks, Christopher, and Meredith Phillips, eds. 1998. *The Black-White Test Score Gap.* Washington, DC: Brookings Institution Press.

Jencks, Christopher, Marshall Smith, Henry Acland, Mary Jo Bane, David Cohen, Herbert Gintis, Barbara Heyns, and Stephanie Michelson. 1972. *Inequality: A Reassessment of the Effect of Family and Schooling in America.* New York, NY: Harper Colophon Books.

Johnson, William R., and Derek Neal. 1998. "Basic Skills and the Black-White Earnings Gap." In *The Black-White Test Score Gap,* edited by Christopher Jencks and Meredith Phillips, 480–500. Washington, DC: Brookings Institution Press.

Joshi, Ela, Sy Doan, and Matthew G. Springer. 2018. "Student-Teacher Race Congruence: New Evidence and Insight From Tennessee." *AERA Open* 4 (4): 233285841881752.

Kantor, Harvey, and Robert Lowe. 2013. "Educationalizing the Welfare State and Privatizing Education: The Evolution of Social Policy Since the New Deal." In *Closing the Opportunity Gap,* edited by P. L. Carter and K. G. Welner, 25–39. New York, NY: Oxford University Press.

Katz, Michael. 2013. *Public Education under Siege.* Philadelphia: University of Pennsylvania Press.

Kenworthy, Lane. 2014. "America's Social Democratic Future: The Arc of Policy Is Long but Bends Toward Justice." *Foreign Affairs* 93 (1): 86–100.

Kingston, Paul W. 2001. "The Unfulfilled Promise of Cultural Capital Theory." *Sociology of Education,* 74, special issue, *Current of Thought: Sociology of Education at the Dawn of the 21st Century*: 88–99.

Kotlowitz, Alex. 2015. "'The Prize,' by Dale Russakoff." *New York Times,* August 19. https://www.nytimes.com/2015/08/23/books/review/the-prize-by-dale-russakoff.html?searchResultPosition=1.

Kozol, Jonathan. 1991. *Savage Inequalities: Children in America's Schools*. New York: Harper Perennial.

Lareau, Annette, and Kimberly A. Goyette. 2014. *Choosing Homes, Choosing Schools*. New York, NY: Russell Sage Foundation.

Levanon, A., P. England, and P. Allison. 2009. "Occupational Feminization and Pay: Assessing Causal Dynamics Using 1950–2000 U.S. Census Data." *Social Forces* 88 (2): 865–91.

Massey, Douglas S. 1995. "The Bell Curve: Intelligence and Class Structure in American Life. Richard J. Herrnstein , Charles Murray." *American Journal of Sociology* 101 (3): 747–53.

Massey, Douglas S., and Robert J. Sampson. 2009. "Moynihan Redux: Legacies and Lessons." *Annals of the American Academy of Political and Social Science* 621 (1): 6–27.

McCall, Leslie. 2013. *The Undeserving Rich: American Beliefs about Inequality, Opportunity, and Redistribution*. Cambridge: Cambridge University Press.

Medina, Jennifer. 2010. "Teachers Set Deal With City on Discipline Process." *New York Times*. Retrieved January 21, 2020. https://www.nytimes.com/2010/04/16/nyregion/16rubber.html?searchResultPosition=1.

Merry, Joseph J. 2013. "Tracing the U.S. Deficit in PISA Reading Skills to Early Childhood: Evidence from the United States and Canada." *Sociology of Education* 86 (3): 234–52.

Millard, Maria, and Stephanie Aragon. 2015. *State Funding for Students with Disabilties: All States All Data*. Denver, CO: Education Commission of the States.

Moynihan, Daniel Patrick, Lee Rainwater, and William L. Yancey. 1967. *The Negro Family: The Case for National Action*. Cambridge, MA: MIT Press.

National Association for Gifted Children. 2015. *State of the States in Gifted Education: Policy and Practice Data*. Washington, DC.

National Center for Education Statistics. 2010. "The Condition of Education: Public School Expenditures by District Poverty (Indicator 36-2010)." Washington, DC: U.S. Department of Education.

National Center for Education Statistics. 2012. "Digest of Education Statistics." Retrieved June 28, 2012. http://nces.ed.gov/programs/coe/indicator_pri.asp.

National Center for Education Statistics. 2017. *Digest of Education Statistics, 2017*. Washington, DC: U.S. Department of Education.

Ohio Department of Education. 2019. *Understanding Ohio's School Report Card*. http://education.ohio.gov/getattachment/Topics/Data/Report-Card-Resources/Sections/General-Report-Card-Information/A-F-Report-Card.pdf.aspx.

Piketty, Thomas. 2014. *Capital in the Twenty-First Century*. Cambridge, MA: Belknap Press of Harvard University Press.

Quinn, D. M., N. Cooc, J. McIntyre, and C. J. Gomez. 2016. "Seasonal Dynamics of Academic Achievement Inequality by Socioeconomic Status and Race/Ethnicity: Updating and Extending Past Research With New National Data." *Educational Researcher* 45 (8): 443–53.

Rawls, John. 1999. *A Theory of Justice*. Rev. ed. Cambridge, MA: Belknap Press of Harvard University Press.

Reardon, Sean F. 2011. "The Widening Academic Achievement Gap Between the Rich and the Poor: New Evidence and Possible Explanations." In *Whither Opportunity: Rising Inequality, Schools, and Children's Life Chances*, edited by Greg J. Duncan and Richard J. Murnane, 91–116. New York: Russell Sage Foundation.

Renzulli, Linda A., and Vincent J. Roscigno. 2005. "Charter School Policy, Implementation, and Diffusion across the United States." *Sociology of Education* 78 (4): 344.

Ropeik, David. 2010. "Global Warming: No Big Deal?" *The Atlantic*. Retrieved January 6, 2020 https://www.theatlantic.com/technology/archive/2010/03/global-warming-no-big-deal/36835/.

Rothstein, Richard. 2004. *Class and Schools: Using Social, Economic, and Educational Reform to Close the Black-White Achievement Gap*. Washington, DC: Economic Policy Institute and Teachers College.

Russakoff, Dale. 2015. "The Prize: Who's in Charge of America's Schools?" New York, NY: Houghton Mifflin Harcourt.

Ryan, William. 1971. *Blaming the Victim*. New York, NY: Pantheon Books.

Sampson, Robert J., Patrick Sharkey, and Stephen W. Raudenbush. 2008. "Durable Effects of Concentrated Disadvantage on Verbal Ability among African-American Children." *Proceedings of the National Academy of Sciences of the United States of America* 105 (3): 845–52.

Schneider, Barbara. 2018. "Introduction." in *Handbook of the Sociology of Education in the 21st Century*, xvii. New York, NY: Springer.

Schneider, Jack. 2016. "Small Schools: The Edu-Reform Failure That Wasn't." *Education Week*, February 9.

Schwartz, Heather. 2010. "Housing Policy Is School Policy: Economically Integrative Housing Promotes Academic Success in Montgomery County, Maryland." In *The Future of School Integration*, edited by Richard D. Kahlenberg. New York, NY: Century Foundation.

Shonkoff, Jack P., and Andrew S. Garner. 2012. "The Lifelong Effects of Early Childhood Adversity and Toxic Stress." *Pediatrics* 129 (1): e232–e346.

Sopolsky, Robert M. 2017. *Behave: The Biology of Humans at Our Best and Worst.* New York, NY: Penguin Books.

Specia, Megan. 2017. "'Frida Sofia': The Mexico Earthquake Victim Who Never Was." *New York Times*, September 27.

Steffes, Tracy Lynn. 2012. *School, Society, and State: A New Education to Govern Modern America, 1890–1940.* Chicago, IL: University of Chicago Press.

Thum, Yeow Meng. 2018. "The Vertical, Interval Scale Assumption of a Computerized Adaptive Test: Evidence from Additive Conjoint Measurement." in *ITC Meetings.* Montreal, Canada.

Tyack, David B., and Larry Cuban. 1995. *Tinkering toward Utopia: A Century of Public School Reform.* Cambridge, MA: Harvard University Press.

von Hippel, Paul T. 2010. "Schools and Inequality, Revisited." Unpublished dissertation, Department of Sociology, Ohio State University,Columbus, Ohio.

von Hippel, Paul T. 2016. "Year-Round School Calendars: Effects on Summer Learning, Achievement, Families, and Teachers." In *Summer Learning and Summer Learning Loss: Theory, Research, and Practice*, edited by K. L. Alexander, M. Boulay, and S. Pitcock. New York: Teachers College Press.

von Hippel, Paul T., and Caitlin Hamrock. 2019. "Do Test Score Gaps Grow Before, During, or between the School Years? Measurement Artifacts and What We Can Know in Spite of Them." *Sociological Science* 6 (3): 43–80.

von Hippel, Paul T., Brian Powell, Douglas B. Downey, and Nicholas J. Rowland. 2007. "The Effect of School on Overweight in Childhood: Gain in Body Mass Index during the School Year and during Summer Vacation." *American Journal of Public Health* 97 (4): 696–702.

von Hippel, Paul T., and Joseph Workman. 2016. "From Kindergarten Through Second Grade, U.S. Children's Obesity Prevalence Grows Only During Summer Vacations." *Obesity* 24 (11): 2296–300.

von Hippel, Paul T., Joseph Workman, and Douglas B. Downey. 2018. "Inequality in Reading and Math Skills Forms Mainly before Kindergarten: A Replication, and Partial Correction, of 'Are Schools the Great Equalizer?'" *Sociology of Education* 9 (4): 323–57.

Walberg, Herbert J. 1984. "Families As Partners in Educational Productivity." *Phi Delta Kappan* 65 (6): 397–400.

Walters, Pam. 1995. "Crisis in Excllence and Social Order in American Education: A Historical Perspective." In *Educational Advance-*

ment and Distributive Justice: Between Equality and Equity, edited by R. Kahane. Jerusalem: The Magnes Press.

Whitehurst, Grover J. "Russ." 2016. *Family Support or School Readiness? Contrasting Models of Public Spending on Children's Early Care and Learning*. Washington, DC: Brookings Institution.

Zuberi, Dan. 2006. *Differences That Matter: Social Policy and the Working Poor in the United States and Canada*. Ithaca, NY: ILR Press/Cornell University Press.

INDEX

Page numbers in italics indicate figures.

ability grouping, 69–70, 72, 87, 110
achievement gaps, 2, 5–7, 9–10, 58–60, 74–75, 81, 96–97, 111, 118, 141n10; formed prior to kindergarten, 15–16, 27, 98, 119; race-based, 6, 40 (*see also* black/white gaps); SES-based, 17, *20*, 28, 38–40, *39*, 71, 92, 109–10, 120, 149n10
achievement tests, 115
Advanced Placement classes, 54, 56, 69, 120–21
Alcaraz, Melissa, 59, 134
Alexander, Karl, 2–3, 9, 109
American Dream, 27, 103, 124
American values: equal opportunity, 9, 110, 125; individualism, 102–3, 147n5; small government, 98, 101–3, 108
Americans with Disabilities Act (1990), 88
Anderson, Cami, 113
Anyon, Jean, 68

Ballou, Dale, 133
Beginning School Study (Baltimore), 21
behavioral expectations, 68–69
Berliner, David C., 141n8
Biddle, Bruce J., 141n8

Bill and Melinda Gates Foundation, 111–12
black families, 104–7
black/white gaps, 39–41, 43, 54–55, 65, 75, 77, 82, 143n6, 143n10. *See also* achievement gaps: race-based
blaming the victim, 98, 103–7
body mass index (BMI), 57, 92
Booker, Corey, 112
Borman, Geoffrey, 145n2
Bourdieu, Pierre, 89
Bowles, Samuel, 68
brain development, 23–24
bullying, 143n14
Burkam, David T., 33

capitalism, 102
causation, in research, 47, 49, 90
Chan, Priscilla, 113
charter schools, 1, 75
Chetty, Raj, 58, 61, 72
child/adult ratio, at home, 85–86
Children in America's Schools (film), 3
class size, 84, 110, 148n16
climate change, 101
cognitive skills, 54–55, 57, 66–67, 91–92, 96, 133–34
Coleman, James, 8, 66, 93, 145n2